VOICES
OF THE
BLACK
THEATRE

VOICES OF

Ruby Dee

Abram Hill

Eddie Hunter

Paul Robeson

Dick Campbell

Vinnette Carroll

Frederick O'Neal

Regina M. Andrews

THE BLACK THEATRE

BY

LOFTEN MITCHELL

JAMES T. WHITE & COMPANY

CLIFTON, NEW JERSEY

Library of Congress Cataloging in Publication Data

Mitchell, Loften.
Voices of the Black theatre.

Contains taped individual recollections of black
theatrical figures with introductory essays and
comments by L. Mitchell.
Includes index.
PARTIAL CONTENTS: The words of Eddie Hunter.—
The words of Regina M. Andrews.—The words of Dick
Campbell. [etc.]
1. Theater—United States.   2. Negro actors.
3 American drama—Negro authors—History and criticism.   I. Title.
PN2286.M5   792'.028'0922   74-30081

ISBN 0-88371-006-4

To the memory of my mother and my father

C O N T E N T S

Theatre is a testament to the life and vitality of a people, one of the things which proves not only that we exist, but that our existence is something unique. Black people have had as long a tradition in theatre as we have had in music and in dance, and that tradition, like the black church, has been one of the things that held us together as a people— it kept us from going mad.

Loften Mitchell is of the heart and soul of that black tradition. He was there. He participated. He was a mover. It is hard to imagine theatre in Harlem at all without him. Loften as usual has done us all a service here; in this book, he has caught it all before it died—or was forgotten.

And it is all here: the names, the dates, the places. The history of a time, a place, a people. A people determined to make their own history, to create their own life style—and thereby not to be destroyed. *Voices of the Black Theatre* is a treasury, a precious repository, a catalogue of our common gifts and talents. A reminder that we, too, are creators—that we too have had and still have something rich and wonderful to say: to ourselves and to all the world. Nobody could have told it so well as Loften. And for that we—all of us—are eternally in his debt.

OSSIE DAVIS

VOICES
OF THE
BLACK
THEATRE

A PERSONAL NOTE ON HOW
THIS BOOK CAME INTO BEING

Professional writers face grave, vexing problems. One of the most devastating of these is that question asked years after a work has appeared:

"What did you mean and why did you write this?"

I intend to meet that problem head on and state now how this book came into being. I intend to do it now. I am tired of paraphrasing Robert Browning: "When I wrote that only God and Robert Browning knew what I was writing. Now, only God knows!"

The roots of this book spread into the summer of 1972. That season roared in on the wings of flood, inflation, Vietnam, crime, and physical and spiritual poverty. The wings dipped down, lashing my face and scarring my very being.

This was a tough summer that followed a tough year. I had spent most of the year writing a screenplay and rewriting a novel. Then, I taught summer school at the State University of New York at Binghamton. I drove up on Mondays from my home in the metropolitan area, lived in the home of that eminent choreographer, Percival Borde, then drove home on Fridays.

Particularly, this was for me the summer of the floods and of the planting of the seeds that sprouted into the roots for this volume.

The floods roared over Elmira, Tioga County and Northeastern Pennsylvania. Houses floated down from place to place and helpless human beings cried out in disaster. Tears flowed down my cheeks for I knew the meaning of homelessness. I knew, indeed, for how many times had I written about being a long, long way from 125th Street?

I gathered my belongings and I stuck my typewriter into my car and I pointed the nose of that car toward New York City. I was tired of seeing human beings suffer. I needed a rest. I was going to hang out, loaf, fish, follow baseball, sit around and gab with my woman, take my children and my grandson fishing, and I was going to party! Yes, indeed! I had my summer planned and nothing was going to interfere—except death.

But, it was not to be. In short, my joyous plans went up in smoke. And the fire that caused this smoke was gradual, indeed. I did go fishing and I caught *nothing*. Meantime, my lady—who had never been fishing before in her life—pulled up two fish!

If you haven't turned the pages yet, bear with me. For things went from bad to worse. I saw some ball games on television and the Yankees and Mets lost. I did party, but—because I was driving—I did not drink. I did see my grandson, but he had hurt his hand and was temporarily hospitalized. I put some money in his piggy bank and somehow or other that little cat figured I owed him five dollars. Furthermore, he went around telling people about it. When I went down to 125th Street one day, a friend walked up to me and asked:

"Why in the hell don't you pay your grandson the five dollars you owe him?"

The smoke was rising, rising.

The smoke really got into my eyes when actor-singer Brock Peters telephoned me to state that he wanted a script written for a show to benefit Arthur Mitchell's Dance Theatre of Harlem. This show was to be called *Come Back to Harlem* (later *Harlem Homecoming*) and to be lavishly produced for a performance at the renovated Loew's Victoria on 125th Street. Lena Horne, Leontyne Price, Cab Calloway and other stars had agreed to appear in it. Apollo Theatre manager Honi Coles was serving as producer. Brock told me that everyone in Harlem had agreed that I was the man to write this script. I was, of course, flattered, not knowing that he was giving me a "snow job." Nor did I realize this until much, much later when I asked about an item known as an honorarium. Brock gave me his big smile and reminded me this was a benefit. Three hundred and seventy-six dollars later I had completed the script, but there was still no loafing.

By then it was high summer of 1972. July had gone and August stared down upon this land. It was high summer, all right, yet somehow there was a trace of fall suggested by the breeze. It was high summer but somehow one sensed the approach of autumn and harvest time and there was the eternal question rearing its head:

"What kind of harvest shall we reap?"

The answer came in staccato fashion: Seymour Peck, editor of the *New York Times* Sunday Arts and Leisure Section reprinted an article I had written about Paul Robeson for Actors' Equity Association—an article suggested by the union's president, Frederick O'Neal. The article appeared on the front page of the August 6, 1972, issue, and now the smoke choked me, for the leaves of summer were turning a golden brown and they, too, were in flames. For one thing, I was not happy to earn publicity from writing about Mr. Robeson's tragic fate. For another thing, the article was published on the birthday of my late mother. And for still another thing, the distinguished pastor of the Church of Our Saviour of Yonkers, Nathaniel T. Grady, Sr., was busy talking me into allowing a production of my play, *Tell Pharaoh*—a production to be directed by

Billy Reed and to star Frederick O'Neal, Hilda Simms, Mubarak Antar Mahmoud, Michelle Stent, Albert Grant, Bertha Jarvis and pianist Earl Gordon. The play came off well, but there was more on the way.

The Reverend Mr. Grady is a doer. He decided to present Ossie Davis in readings from my work. Theatrical veteran Dick Campbell was scheduled to introduce Ossie. But Mr. Grady did not stop at that. He asked the lovely Gwen Hall of Yonkers' *Herald Statesman* to have something written about me. And so a lovely young reporter interviewed me and her story and my picture appeared on page 2 of the newspaper. And my creditors caught up with me. That is another reason why I dislike publicity—plus the fact that I believe a writer should be writing, not sitting before television cameras or collecting clippings.

By this time I was willing to return to my citadel of loneliness in Binghamton. And I did so on the very night that *Harlem Homecoming* was presented. After all, I had seen the show and, besides, there was an important football game on television that night.

But, most of all, I wanted to be alone and sit and think and organize what few days I had left here under the sun and stars. I had long known that I would be forever homeless, that I was a Gypsy man from Harlem, left in this wide world to roam. No thoughts had I of tomorrow except to make heaven my home. . . But heaven is a state of being and the very state of being is at most temporary and transitory. Scarce, indeed, are those who truly care about the state of another human being.

While pondering over all of this, I looked through my mail. And I cried. Stacks of letters stood on my desk, all about the Paul Robeson article. My office had been closed all summer and so I sat down and tried to answer as many letters as I could, yet many remain unanswered to this date.

One particular letter intrigued me. That one came from the editor-in-chief of James T. White and Company, a publishing firm located in Clifton, New Jersey. The next thing I knew this Harlem Gypsy was driving to Clifton and having lunch with the publisher and his editorial department—and having a ball.

Their enthusiasm was a beam of sunlight. Before I knew it, I had agreed to write another book and, being a playwright, it is a matter of record that I had sworn off writing books.

But I am a child of the theatre and when the company decided to call on Eddie Hunter, Dick Campbell, Abram Hill and Frederick O'Neal to appear for a taping session, the ham in me could not be kept packaged inside my being.

We had our taping session in late 1972 and we were fed and paid. We had too much fun to even do any serious drinking. Eddie Hunter told his story from the 1900's into the 1920's. Dick Campbell covered the 1920's and 1930's. Abram Hill told of the 1940's and the early 1950's. Frederick O'Neal then told his story with special emphasis upon his attempts to gain employment for all ethnic groups. It was a great session, beautifully described in Eddie Hunter's statement: "Man, that's *Class!*"

Subsequently, conversations were recorded with Regina M. Andrews, Ruby Dee and Vinnette Carroll.

In reviewing this work, I find there are two major matters that should be stated here. One is about the various Harlem libraries. It is important to note that three libraries existed in the Harlem area that were community-minded. These offered more than the lending of books. They were gathering places for community groups and they held concerts and lectures and provided other educational features. These three were the 135th Street Library, the 124th Street Library, and the 115th Street Library. The 135th Street Library, just off Lenox Avenue, was the scene of the activities of several important black theatre undertakings. Housed now in this structure is the famous Schomburg collection. Mr. Ernest Kaiser, long a member of the Schomburg's staff, has graciously supplied the following note:

> *The basis of the Schomburg Center for Research in Black Culture was the large, important private library on blacks collected by Arthur A. Schomburg (1874-1938), a Puerto Rican of African descent who lived in New York City. A Harlem citizens' committee persuaded the Carnegie Corporation in 1926 to buy Schomburg's library for the New York Public Library and place it in a branch in the heart of Harlem.*
>
> *Recently, the Schomburg Center has become a part of the Research Libraries of the New York Public Library. It has outgrown its quarters and plans are underway for the eventual construction of a new building for the Center near the old site. After much deterioration, conservation of the various materials is proceeding with financial help from several sources.*
>
> *Today the Center consists of 55,000 to 60,000 volumes (with some 50 percent about*

Africa), art objects, musical recordings, photographs, prints, sheet music, manuscripts, scrapbooks, pamphlets, playbills, programs, newspaper clippings, magazine articles, black newspaper files (mostly on microfilm) and runs of black periodicals. The manuscript holdings are extensive. They include the papers of Hiram Revels, Pauli Murray, the National Negro Congress, the Civil Rights Congress, Bessye J. Bearden, the National Association of Colored Graduate Nurses, the Negro Labor Committee, William Pickens and many others. A Calendar of the Manuscripts in the Schomburg Collection of Negro Literature and History, *compiled by the Historical Records Survey, Works Projects Administration, New York City, in 1942, was published by Andronicus Publishing Co., New York, in 1970. The big, nine-volume* Dictionary Catalog of the Schomburg Collection of Negro Literature and History *was published by G. K. Hall in Boston in 1962 with a two-volume first supplement in 1967 and a four-volume second supplement in 1972.*

The 135th Street Library occupies a unique place in black history. Few, indeed, are the articles, books and plays dealing with the black experience that could have been written without the existence of the Schomburg collection. One of its curators was the eminent Lawrence Reddick, and as of this writing Mrs. Jean Blackwell Hutson serves as curator.

The 124th Street Library was located just off Fifth Avenue, facing Mt. Morris Park. Here the Rose

McClendon Players produced plays in the basement theatre. The 115th Street People's Theatre produced shows in the library basement at 203 West 115th Street. Similar activities took place at the 145th Street and 155th Street Libraries, but those were not within the experience of this writer.

The introductory essays and the comments in this volume all flow from the voice of this writer. This book most emphatically does not purport to be an encyclopedic survey of the black theatre. It is, rather, a book of individual recollections brought together to express and portray the flavor and circumstances of one significant aspect of the American theatre in the twentieth century. The essence of this cannot be captured in an encyclopedic work.

Indeed, the subject matter is so vast that it would take many, many volumes to cover in an encyclopedia.

A NOTE

*Special gratitude is offered to the following
for assistance in preparing this work:
Gladys and Herman Blair, Percival Borde,
Pearl Primus, James V. Hatch, Camille
Billops, Honi Coles, Joan K. Whiting, Rosetta
LeNoire, Billie Allen, Jewdyer Osborne, Avon
Long, Frieda Presberg, Alma John, Eugene
Callender, Alice L. Mitchell, and Ted Shine.
The cooperation extended by Jean Blackwell
Hutson and Ernest Kaiser of Harlem's famous
Schomburg Collection was—as is the case in
all books of this type—of immeasurable
importance.*

AN ESSAY ON VOICES

NOT HEARD HEREIN

Prior to the 1950's Washington, D.C., was a citadel of jimcrow. It was in the capital of this nation that black Americans who traveled south had to move into the "Colored" train car. To anyone who does not know those days, what that meant was: black folks rode in one train car and white folks in other cars. Water fountains had signs, some marked "Colored" and others marked "White." There were "Colored" sections in movie houses and "White" sections. There were "Colored" schools and "White" schools. In other words, jimcrow was rampant racism and south of Washington there were signs emphasizing this.

Racism in Washington, D.C., however, did not have jimcrow signs, but black people knew which restaurants would serve them and which theatres would admit them. This was a covert type of racism that kept black people out of various key positions and places. As a matter of fact, when the late Adam Clayton Powell first ran for Congress during World War II, this was one of the key issues of his campaign. During a speech at the Golden Gate Ballroom in Harlem in 1943, he said: "If the black man is good enough to drive a tank for Uncle Sam's army, he is good enough to drive a bus or a trolley in Washington, D.C.!"

All of this may seem ludicrous now when we see black men driving buses and trolleys, but it was a stark reality during World War II. Just one example: The Philadelphia local of the Transport Workers Union called a strike because the transit system attempted to upgrade Negroes. The City of Brotherly Love was then one of our great war towns. But, it was paralyzed during the height of World War II. President Franklin D. Roosevelt finally had to send troops into Philadelphia to quell the disturbances. He declared in a nationwide radio address in 1943 that the nation could not fight a war for democracy abroad while its troops were stationed in Philadelphia.

Considerable agitation and legal thrusts eventually brought an end to overt jimcrow and, to some extent, to covert jimcrow. And that leads us back to Washington, D.C., in the 1950's.

The story is told of a black American who walked by a swank restaurant that did not serve black people. He noticed a sign that stated: "As of next week this restaurant will be open to all, regardless of race, creed, color or national origin."

Well, the black man went home and waited for a week. When the week had passed, he went back to the restaurant, seated himself and told the waiter:

"I'll have some chitlins, some corn bread, pig's feet, some yams and collard greens."

The shocked waiter looked at the man and said: "Sir, I'm sorry. We don't have that type of food."

The black man said: "Look man—you had a week to get ready for me! You knew I was coming!"

So it is with this volume. You knew this book was on its way, and you had years and years to get ready for it. In fact, you had three centuries! And even those scholars who know little of the black experience should have known it was on its way—that is, if they know America. If they do know this land, then they know that it is destined to look around at various times and find riches in its midst and suddenly herald the arrival of a New Day, a Time of Awareness, a New Breed! Yet, one look reveals the reality that this New Thing, this New Experience is as old as the nation itself.

And so it is with the black theatre movement.

For those who believe the black theatre movement

started yesterday, a perusal of the works of Sterling A. Brown and James Weldon Johnson will make them think twice. Mr. Brown's fine work in a volume entitled *Negro Poetry and Drama* and his essay in the *Oxford Companion to the Theatre* establish him as a primary figure in the exploration of the black American in the theatre. And Mr. Johnson's *Black Manhattan* further documents the reality that the black theatre is no new phenomenon in America. That great Rhodes scholar, Dr. Alain Locke, has also made numerous brilliant comments on the black theatre.

And this volume further demonstrates this reality by allowing a group of pioneers to tell their stories in their own words. Here, it must be added that no single volume can include all the names and contributors to the black theatre movement. To look at this work "to see if my name or my friends' names are included" is to use the wrong approach to a subject that is greater than personalities. And black theatre is, indeed, greater than the sum of its parts.

To understand fully the stories told in these pages, an overview of more than three hundred years is mandatory. This overview demands the rejection of various myths and half-truths that have been paraded throughout Western world history. This overview is not going to be pleasant to those who desire to rearrange their prejudices or justify the fact that a New Idea has appeared. In short, there are people of all groups who are not going to like it, but if we are to seek the truth, then we must deal with human beings as human beings, not as man-sculptured gods and goddesses.

This overview begins with the reality that Middle Ages Europe was an impoverished land, trade-less, seeking new horizons. Then Marco Polo and his adventurers brought lurid tales of endless Oriental wealth. And it is said by many—including John Henrik Clarke in *Harlem U.S.A.* and J. A. Rogers in *Africa's Gift to America*—that Columbus learned of a land to the west from his contact with Africans. The Africanesque features of many ancient Latin American art objects suggest that Africans touched the American continent long, long before Columbus.

It is a matter of record, however, that one of Columbus' ships was captained by a man of African origin named Pietro. There was also a black man with Ponce de Leon when he "discovered" Florida and one with Balboa when he "discovered" the Pacific. Contrary to the lies of history, black people were in the New World long before the first slaves arrived at Jamestown in 1619.

In 1626 when New York City was a Dutch outpost known as New Amsterdam, black people were very much in evidence. Peter Stuyvesant declared: "All is well, thanks to the employment of Negroes." When he left for Holland, he wrote: "Let the company's Negroes keep good watch on my Bowery!"

In short, slavery in the New World was "integrated." Black people and white people were indentured servants and slavery was a matter of labor, not color. In fact, there are records showing that well-to-do black people owned slaves. The British conquest of New Amsterdam in 1664 led to the introduction of chattel slavery. A badge was placed on color and the black man's visibility marked him as the man who was going to be betrayed in the search for the American Dream.

This was apparent when the nation was founded. The so-called founding fathers ignored landless whites when they founded this nation. And they considered black people "three-fifths human." The American Revolution was fought to keep the British from getting a "piece of the action," namely, profits. It was also fought to determine who had the *right* to battle the red people for the land. Yet, the war was fought, led by a slaveholder, urged on by another slaveholder who shouted: "Give me liberty or give me death!"

And one of the ironies of history is that more than five thousand black men and black women fought in that war and helped to turn the tide of the American Revolution.

Why?

Were they really naive? Were the red people naive when they welcomed the white people and taught them to grow corn? Why, indeed? And speculation can only enter here. The black man, like the red man, was community-minded, believing that all belong to the land and the land to all. The appearance of a stranger brought an open invitation to him to join the community and partake of all that was there. The suspicion cannot be avoided that the European stranger had been so victimized by greed and lust, so thoroughly impoverished, so deprived that he had to seize everything within sight—to commit what we snidely refer to today as "crime in the streets."

Indeed, the relationship of the enslaving, colonizing Europeans of those times directly parallels the present-day war between the "have-nots" and the "haves." The black, red, Latin and other groups who seek riches in the midst of their own impoverishment—or a "piece of the action"—have had examples set by former slaveholders, pirates and colonizers.

These matters are discussed in the Clarke and

Rogers books, *Black Manhattan*, and my *Tell Pharoah*.

At any rate, the black reality was Africa and then America and the islands of the sea were seized. Yet— the eighteenth century brought dreams about the Rights of Man, of Liberty, Equality and Fraternity. And these dreams burned bright in the hearts of black people. How else can one explain Phillis Wheatley's lines of verse to General George Washington? How else can one explain Phoebe Fraunces saving the life of Washington when an Irish traitor named Hickey tried to poison him? How else can one explain Phoebe's father, Sam Fraunces, giving up a lucrative restaurant business and joining the staff of President Washington? Works by Johnson, Clarke, Lerone Bennett, Gertrude McBrown, and by Dr. W. E. B. DuBois discuss these questions relating to the dreams. But further:

How else, indeed, does one explain the so-called black revolution of the 1950's and 1960's which—like it or not—was a reform movement, a movement to "get in the system" rather than basically change it?

The black American has bought the American Dream! And he was an early "buyer," a true believer, waiting, hoping, dreaming of the day when the Dream would be a reality. Indeed, he became defensive about his right to dream, pleading, cajoling, trying to prove himself worthy of his God-given rights. He was forced into a defensive position and had to prove "We are not all lazy. We are not all thieves. We are not all murderers. We are just like white folks!"

The black American had to cry when he should have yelled, yell when he should have cried, prove himself worthy in the company of the worthless, spend man-hours debating about approaches to freedom and become a victim of endless *etceteras* while being denied ordinary human frailties. He had to be a super-Negro in order to survive. And all the while a system was being rigged against him—a system that was to keep him on the defensive, keep him apologetic, impoverished and keep him gathering crumbs from beneath the table of Plenty. And all of this was because his misery made others rich.

The theatre illustrates this in sharp, significant terms. And—while this is a reality in terms of black theatre—it is also a reality in terms of poor black life, poor white life, poor Mexican life, poor Indian life, poor Latin life, and poor Oriental life.

But, here we are discussing black theatre and once again we are grateful to Sterling A. Brown for his documentation. He has told us that in the eighteenth century the American theatre attempted to deal realistically with black people in *The Fall of British Tyranny* (1776). In that play black slaves were offered freedom by the British if they joined in fighting against the Yankee upstarts in the American Revolution. Many did, including some of George Washington's own slaves, and the British later freed them and settled them in Nova Scotia, where their descendants live now. But, the tone set there was not to last. Murdock's *The Triumph of Love* in 1795 introduced a shuffling, cackling "darky" and the rape of the black image had begun.

Bold attempts were made thereafter to laugh at the Negro's features, his habits, his very being. He was a creature to be scorned, humiliated, assailed from pulpits and public lecterns. Yes. He was on the defensive—a position he occupies to this very day. And this defensive position led to some extremely interesting cultural activities. One thing it led to was the forgotten fact that the theatre is not necessarily *white*. Chinese and Japanese works illustrate that. And there is another fact and that is that a man of African ancestry named Alexandre Dumas, *fils*, author of *Camille*, was responsible for what came to be known as the "well-made play."

Another forgotten reality that led to a defensive position for blacks was the creation and development of minstrelsy. Sometime during the eighteenth century black slaves on southern plantations created the minstrel form. This form—the forerunner of the American musical comedy pattern—was designed by slaves to satirize slavemasters. The first half of the performance had a group of at least seventeen men, all elaborately costumed, their faces blackened with burnt cork. These men sat in a half circle. At the center was the interlocutor, or master of ceremonies, a "straight man," who fed jokes to the comedians and was the butt of their replies. On the other side of the master of ceremonies were at least seven singers, dancers, monologuists, or other featured performers. At the end of each line were the "end men," Mr. Bones and Tambo, so named for the instruments they played. The bones were used like castanets, and Tambo had a tambourine. Bones and Tambo were the leading comics. A band was in the orchestra pit or seated behind the performers. Each performance began with the interlocutor stating: "Gentlemen, be seated!" Ballads, comic songs, dialogues and dances followed in quick succession and a "walk around" brought the first half to a close. The second half was an olio. This was the less traditional form, more like burlesque and vaudeville shows with sketches in which all the players were male.

Of this Sterling Brown wrote in his essay "The Negro in the American Theatre" *(Oxford Companion)*: "Though black-face minstrelsy started out with rudimentary realism, it soon degenerated into fantastic artificiality." It should be noted here that the reason for this degeneration grew out of northern white troubadors visiting southern plantations, witnessing minstrelsy, copying it and blackening their faces. What black slaves had conceived as a satiric form was taken from them and *used against them!*

Mr. Brown documents this further: "It must be remembered that Ethiopian minstrelsy was white masquerade; Negro performers were not allowed to appear in it until after the Civil War; it was composed by whites, acted and sung by whites in burnt cork for white audiences. It succeeded in fixing one stereotype deeply in the American consciousness: the shiftless, lazy, improvident, loud-mouthed, flashily dressed Negro with kinky hair and large lips, over-addicted to the eating of watermelon and chicken (almost always purloined), the drinking of gin, the shooting of dice, and the twisting of language into ludicrous malformations. Life was a perennial joke or 'breakdown.' Black-face minstrelsy underestimated and misrepresented the American Negro in much the same way that the English drama treated the stage Irishman."

In the nineteenth century, specifically in 1820, a black tragedian, James Hewlett, spearheaded the founding of the African Grove Theatre in New York City. This theatre, located at Bleecker and Grove Streets, performed the classics for free Negroes. The African Grove was the source of inspiration for the great actor, Ira Aldridge. But, the police harassed the company, often arresting actors in the middle of a performance. The actors returned after being released from jail and they performed again—until the next arrest. White hoodlums also created disturbances in the theatre and the management was compelled to post a sign, asking whites to sit in the rear of the theatre because "white people do not know how to behave at entertainment designed for ladies and gentlemen of color."

White hoodlums eventually wrecked the African Grove. With its destruction the great Ira Aldridge realized that America offered little to the black theatre artist. He sailed for Europe where he was acclaimed by royalty. A chair stands now in his honor at Stratford-on-Avon, placed there by black Americans.

It is significant to note that less than two years after Aldridge left these shores, the shuffling, cackling stereotype of black people was acclaimed on the New York stage—projected by a white man in blackface.

Equally significant is that, following the Civil War, the black American appeared in the American theatre as a minstrel man. He became, in the words of James Weldon Johnson, a "caricature of a caricature."

Despite the continued destructive effects of the minstrel tradition, black playwrights came into a measure of prominence long before the Civil War. Henry Brown, one of the founders of the African Grove, is said to have been a playwright. Outside of actor Ira Aldridge, who wrote the *Black Doctor* (1847) and Victor Séjour, author of *The Brown Overcoat* (1858), possibly the best known black playwright was William Wells Brown, author of *The Escape; or A Leap to Freedom* (1858). William Lloyd Garrison wrote in *The Liberator* of the playwright's power and eloquence.

William Wells Brown was born into slavery. He escaped from slavery and became an eloquent, fiery voice against that institution. He spoke at rallies, in private homes, at gatherings and before the Abolitionists, slashing away at the evil known as chattel slavery. Many academicians have had much to say of Brown's written work, particularly *The Escape; or A Leap to Freedom.* Some have been brazen enough to speak of it in condescending terms, claiming that it has dramaturgical holes and lacks theatricality. Well, for anyone who reads Brown's work without bias, one cold reality looms visibly before all: The work is on the level of most dramatic material written during that era. And for fire, conviction and sincerity, it is better than most of the work of the time.

Despite Brown's work and that of other anti-slavery writers—including Mrs. Harriet Beecher Stowe with her *Uncle Tom's Cabin*—minstrelsy remained a dominant theatrical force. After the Civil War black entertainers participated in minstrel shows and became, indeed, caricatures of a caricature. James Bland, composer of "Carry Me Back to Old Virginny" and "In the Evening by the Moonlight," was a prominent minstrel man. However, the rage of discontent that simmered in the hearts of those who lived the black experience for many, many years now erupted openly. And the rage only came openly when reactionary forces grouped and plotted to sell the Negro back into slavery by putting on him a badge of color, by feeding jimcrow and cheap wages to poor whites and dividing and conquering the common men of both races.

It was all done swiftly, quickly, expertly. Northern industrialists and Southern plantation owners conspired to divide the poor white and the poor black. True, the War between the States was followed by a period known as Reconstruction—a period when a large majority of black men and white men in the South lived like decent human beings. There existed the Freedmen's Bureau to assist those slaves who had been freed with just the rags on their backs. There were Union Army soldiers in the Southland to protect the freed men. And there were more black political figures in the various legislatures than we have at the time of this writing. Although oppressive forces seethed, it was a time of democracy, a time that that great scholar, W. E. B. DuBois, spoke of in his book, *Black Reconstruction*, as "The Coming of the Lord."

But—freedom means freedom for every man, woman and child and greedy, onerous forces were unwilling to permit large groups of poor blacks and poor whites to enjoy this freedom. Freedom, after all, cuts into profits and the organized conspiracy of the greedy sold the common man back into slavery—black slavery and white slavery. But, this was a pseudo-sophisticated type of slavery named jimcrow. It was programmed by experts. Jimcrow laws appeared on the books of southern legislatures. Negroes were sent to one school and whites to another. Negroes had to sit in the rear of buses and trolley cars and whites had to sit up front. That was the law! And cheap labor was the new form of slavery, buttressed by the color line, enforced by lynch mobs, the Ku Klux Klan, the Night Riders and aided by the communications media. For black Americans were assailed in pulpits, public places, in the press, and in literature, history and theatre.

Many poor whites and blacks fought back, but you don't read about this in American history books or see it on television and movie screens. Bullets poured from guns triggered by black men with whites on their side.

There were cases, too, of black men and women organizing much as they did during the Montgomery bus boycott of the 1950's. They organized into carriage pools and "Gypsy" travel services, but these organizations soon felt the wrath of oppressive forces and were beaten back. And history has hidden the heroic deeds of these men and women. Even a great "liberal" like Senator Jacob Javits can stand up and speak before a Harlem congregation at the Church of the Master as he did and say that, in a sense, what happened during the 1960's was the Negro's fault for waiting one hundred years to fight for his rights! And even modern young blacks and liberal whites have the gall to speak of the new age of Black Awareness!

God cries for their ignorance!

God's tears have rained down upon us for years and years. During the 1940's and 1950's black playwrights Abram Hill, George Norford, Theodore Ward, Theodore Browne, Louis Peterson, Alice Childress, William Branch, Lorraine Hansberry and this writer had to fight off salutes to the new Negro playwright, the black playwright who had "come of age"!

Had anyone cared to look into history, he might have discovered the heroic deeds of such black theatrical pioneers as Bert Williams, George Walker, Jesse Shipp, Alex Rogers, Bob Cole, J. Rosamond Johnson, Will Marion Cook and Paul Laurence Dunbar. These men—along with others—sat down during the age of racism that existed after the sabotage of the Reconstruction. They sat down in the latter part of the nineteenth century and boldly decided to destroy the minstrel pattern by putting on plays with music. In doing so they created the multimillion-dollar musical production pattern.

And it was no flash in the pan, either. Bob Cole, along with J. Rosamond Johnson, composer of "Lift Every Voice and Sing," wrote the operas *The Red Moon* and *The Shoofly Regiment*. In April, 1898, Cole was represented by a vehicle known as *A Trip to Coontown*, produced at the Third Avenue Theatre. This multitalented young man later housed a stock company at Worth's Museum on Sixth Avenue in the Greenwich Village area. However, he died at an early age and brought despair to black theatregoers. Dunbar and Cook wrote *Clorindy—the Origin of the Cakewalk*; it was particularly well-received. During this era, too, Jesse Shipp and Alex Rogers were creating works for Bert Williams and George Walker. The Williams and Walker company, after a number of "road vehicles," crashed Broadway with an original musical called *In Dahomey*. This work went on to London where it played for a year. It was presented at a Command Performance at Buckingham Palace in the year 1903.

Williams and Walker's next musical, *In Abyssinia*, had a book by Jesse Shipp and Alex Rogers and music by Will Marion Cook. One New York critic brazenly wrote that this musical was "a little too high-brow for a darky show." The work opened with Cook's soaring number, "Song of Reverence to the Setting Sun." The story told of George Walker obtaining a large sum of money and taking Bert Williams and some friends to Abyssinia. There the comic, ragged Bert wandered in and out of royal African settings, all of which beautifully contrasted the conditions of Afro-Americans and Africans.

Williams and Walker's next show, *Bandanna Land*, made even more acidic comments about black-white relationships in the United States. This work, produced in 1908, told of a group of black people who wanted to get rich quick. They bought up land in a white section, raised hell there, then proceeded to sell the land back to the whites at twice the amount the blacks paid for it. If this were not an attack upon the "Negro-scare racket" and "block-busting," one does not exist!

George Walker became ill during the run of *Bandanna Land*. This illness led to his retirement and eventual death. Bert Williams went on alone into *Mr. Lode of Kole*, feeling, in his own words, "like a rudderless ship." *Mr. Lode of Kole* was only a moderate success and after that—because he had no other job—Williams joined the *Follies* at the invitation of producer Abraham Erlanger.

To this writer's knowledge, Bert Williams was the only black artist who worked in the downtown theatre between 1910 and 1917. This feat alone contributed to his early death at the age of 46 in 1922. The tall, proud, literate West Indian did not look like white Americans thought Negroes should. And so, despite his objections, he was compelled to wear burnt cork, to darken his face, and shuffle like a so-called "darky." That great critic, Heywood Broun, declared that Williams' enormous talents were largely neglected. When Williams first joined the *Follies*, Erlanger had a special role written into the show for him. The cast threatened to strike because it did not want to appear on stage with a Negro. A compromise was reached. This called for Williams to appear on stage alone and perform his monologues. And Williams' artistry did the rest. He literally stopped the show. And, of course, the cast very quickly changed its collective thinking and wanted Williams integrated into the show!

Pages could be written about the rank discrimination faced by Williams throughout his career—of riding the freight elevators with the applause still ringing in his ears, of the bartender who wanted to charge him fifty dollars for a drink, of eating alone in his hotel room while on tour, and countless indignities known to all who have lived the black experience in America. This writer's play *Star of the Morning*—written with composer Louis Mitchell and lyricist Romare Bearden, the great artist—deals with much of Williams' early life.

But the point being made here is that black artists were excluded from Broadway between 1910 and 1917 with the exception of Williams. And black people were excluded as patrons.

Nor was this an accident. As previously noted, this period only briefly antedated the time of the sabotage of the Reconstruction Era, the time of the same type of backlash faced by black people today in the United States. The Supreme Court—like all other institutions—was an oracle for white America and rampant racism. The Court's *Plessy v. Ferguson* decision upheld the separate-but-equal doctrine, or jimcrow. The "badge on color" was firmly nailed into American consciousness and hair texture, skin color, and lynching Negroes all made life for black Americans into a bed of misery. The press willingly joined these oppressive forces and in the context of the theatre declared that the "Negro musical comedy is running thin."

Lynch mobs rode the Southern night and race riots flared in cities. During the 1900 race riot in New York City, the white mob yelled: "Get Williams and Walker!" James Weldon Johnson tells in *Black Manhattan* that comedian Ernest Hogan had to lock himself up inside a theatre to hide from the mob. The rape of the black American continued, and his position was, indeed, a defensive one.

The attacks on black people in New York City were merciless. White hoodlums went into black people's homes and beat women and children. Black men coming home from work had to meet other black men on street corners and walk together. My uncle, Hosea Spaulding, and my father, Ulysses Mitchell, were there. They were there and they told me about it as did many other old-time New Yorkers. And it was this type of terror that made many black people welcome the development of the community known as Harlem.

A word must be said about that community. In 1626 eleven African slaves built a wagon road from the fringe of what is now the Bowery to the upper part of New Amsterdam—to a place the Dutch called Haarlem. Eighteen years later, with the support of the rank and file white colonists, these Africans successfully petitioned the Dutch for freedom, then settled in a swampland which they built into a prosperous community. That community is today known as Greenwich Village.

Mid-nineteenth century Harlem was a place peopled by crude squatters who lived in corrugated huts—with the exception of such fashionable places as homes like the one owned by Alexander Hamilton. But the march of what we call progress was under way. Improved lighting, transportation and modern living conditions transformed Harlem into what became New York City's first suburb: Harlem. Harlem, U.S.A.

But this wasn't the Harlem, U.S.A., that we black militants talk about today. This was White Protestant American Harlem! By 1886 three elevated lines reached the community and the elite attempted to escape from the foreign-born who reached American shores. They escaped to Harlem where they built mansions and had horse-drawn carriages. And, oh, it was indeed a center of fashion and culture. Residents were careful to note to friends that they lived in Harlem. The city was for "those foreigners." And Public School 68, which was between Lenox and Seventh Avenues on 128th Street, was called the Silk Stocking School. I know. It was the first school attended by Sister Gladys, Brother Clayton and this writer. We fought with whites on our way to school, in school, and on our way home from school.

How did we get there? Well, in the early part of the twentieth century the news circulated that a Lenox Avenue subway line was being constructed. By 1904 all of Harlem's vacant land had been sold. Houses were built and they stood, waiting to be rented. Wild speculation raged and the bust followed the boom. Black Americans headed off the bust.

They headed it off because the high rents charged for apartments discouraged the general white population. Real estate men were therefore quite willing to rent apartments to home-hungry, harassed black people—especially at two to three times the amount of rental that whites would normally pay. And so the first black Americans moved in and the whites resisted and the black folks fought back and said, boldly, "We are in Harlem to stay!"

Many white Americans fled, but many remained. And they remain until this very day, but you don't see them on television or movie screens. To show respectable whites living beside respectable blacks in the Harlem of this decade would be to put the lie to the notion that Harlem is populated by animals, junkies, welfare clients and dope peddlers. The present-day distorted image of Harlem is deliberately calculated to destroy the community, to reclaim it for upper middle class whites with only a sprinkling of token blacks. For Harlem is the only black community in America that is not out by the railroad tracks. You go *up* to Harlem, not *out* to Harlem. And it is Harlem, not Colored Town, or You-Know-What Town. It is Harlem.

Big, broadbacked, gentle Harlem had four legitimate theatres during the early part of the twentieth century. The Crescent on 135th Street where the Lenox Terrace apartments now stand, the Lincoln, the Lafayette, and the Alhambra. And they put on professional shows, too, and they were second to none.

In 1909 writer-actor-producer Eddie Hunter produced shows at the Crescent, notably *Going to the Races* and *The Battle of Who Run.* This is the same Eddie Hunter who tells his own story in the pages that follow. This is the same Eddie Hunter who wrote the Broadway show *How Come?* Mr. Hunter was not the only artist whose work was presented at the Crescent. Harry Lawrence Freeman's opera, *An African Kraal*, was done there. And near the Lenox Avenue corner stood the Lincoln Theatre where Henry Kramer and S. H. Dudley had their plays produced.

E. S. Wright performed Othello at the Lafayette and in 1913 J. Leubrie Hill's *Darktown Follies* played there. One critic wrote that the first night "looked like a Broadway opening." Producer Florenz Ziegfeld bought the finale of that show for his own *Follies*—the same *Follies* Abraham Erlanger had invited Bert Williams to join. Later at the Lafayette came *Darkydom* by Aubrey Lyles and Flournoy Miller and many of its sketches were sold to Broadway. And Aubrey Lyles and Flournoy Miller were later to meet Noble Sissle and Eubie Blake and write that smash hit, *Shuffle Along*.

Oh, yes! Harlem was singing and swinging, swinging and singing and it is well that we get ready to hear the stories of these pioneers. It is totally fitting and proper that we should know their stories, for I see a hell of an age a-coming!

I see a hell of an age a-coming because the Black American Theatre is a vital, integral part of the American Theatre. I see a hell of an age a-coming when there shall rise the American Indian Theatre, the Latin American Theatre, the Chinese and Japanese Theatre, the Italian Theatre, the Irish Theatre, the Ethnic Theatre.

Oh, yes! I see a hell of an age a-coming because out of these ethnic theatres we shall have men and women from diverse cultures know each other, really know each other and deal with each other as forthright men and women. I see a hell of an age a-coming because the melting-pot theory will be cast aside and men and women will be proud of their individual differences and stand up straight and tall and proud. I see a hell of an age a-coming because these pioneers have plowed the fields and we shall reap a great harvest!

Eddie Hunter is a man who has plowed. I knew him long before he knew me. I saw him in the Harlem theatres during my boyhood. He had a reputation for doing "clean" comedy in an age of "smut." In other words, he didn't resort to sex jokes, race jokes, or bathroom jokes. I got to know him during the writing of my book *Black Drama*. I went to his house for an hour and when I left four hours later I was drunk from his bourbon and his stories.

In 1968 a Harlem cultural group honored him with a presentation for his distinguished service to the Black Theatre. A group of us went to his house and gave him the award. He then wanted to know if we would visit him three months later for his birthday celebration. I shook my head in utter disbelief. He was going on eighty and there I was, forty-seven years old, hoping that I would live until I was forty-eight.

And we went to his party. And I had a ball!

Men like Eddie Hunter make me certain when I say: I see a hell of an age a-coming!

Eddie Hunter

THE WORDS OF
Eddie Hunter

I am Eddie Hunter, born in New York City on 97th Street between Second and Third Avenues on February 4, 1888. I am eighty-four years young.

In 1903 at the age of fifteen I left school to go to work. I had a great desire to write sketches for vaudeville and I had many musical comedy ideas. My best time for writing and thinking was at night from ten on through daybreak. I would light up a cigar and ideas and visions would come to me. Characters would appear. I would direct them with the thoughts that came to my mind and then I would start writing. Sometimes I would find myself laughing at the things I was writing and the things I could see these characters doing.

I took a job as an elevator operator at an apartment house on Madison Avenue. One week I would work from eight in the morning until six at night. The next week I would work the night shift from six in the evening until eight in the morning. It was on the night shift that I would do most of my writing. Most all of the tenants were in by midnight, anyway.

Mr. Enrico Caruso, the great opera singer, often visited in that building. He would talk to me about show business. He always called me "Ed-*ward.*"

One time he said to me: "Why is it whenever I come here and you're on duty, you're always near the elevator. The other fellow is always off somewhere or asleep. With you it's not so. How come?"

I told him I was around because of doing my writing.

He asked: "What're you writing?"

I said: "I'm learning to write plays and sketches."

He said: "Do you mind if I look at the work you're doing?"

I said: "Not at all. That would be an honor to me."

So he looked and he sat there, reading and laughing and amusing himself, and after a half hour he stood up and said:

"Ed-*ward*, keep this up and you won't be running an elevator long."

His words came true. He was my inspiration. He left me with a "Goodnight, Ed-*ward*."

I went back to my writing. And I say it again: Mr. Caruso was my inspiration. Later on, strange as it may seem, the play that I wrote that opened on Broadway in 1923 was titled: *How Come?* He was my inspiration.

The first work I wrote that I recall being produced was in 1905 or 1906. I started writing little sketches and my mother and father—God bless them both, both deceased—would rent a hall and advertise "Entertainment and Dancing" at such-and-such date at such-and-such hall. Then I would put on my work. I would build my own scenery. I would have a curtain stretched across the dance hall when time came for me to put on my show. These shows were hits and after them— on with the dancing. I did that for about two years. Later, this was in New York City at McFarland's Dance Hall, 100th Street and Third Avenue, one flight up. Then in 1910 I went into vaudeville with James Howell. That was my first vaudeville appearance, a team doing comedy acts at the Little Lincoln Theatre. This was a storefront theatre managed by Mr. Frenchy Elmore.

I remember in those days show business was a tough row to hoe, an uphill battle, but I wouldn't give up. I kept fighting. I remember when I worked for forty dollars a week, doing five and six shows a day. Today it is different. A performer makes money today, plenty of money. In my day it was just scraps, crumbs. But, I had to do it and keep forging ahead. I had an agent named Mr. Jack Flynn. He booked me over the cheap circuits and different theatres—Proctor's and other houses. He always said:

"Edward, if you were white, the money I could get for you!"

I said: "Mr. Flynn, I know I am *not* white. Just keep me working and get me money."

So, he would always throw that up to me. He put me in a theatre on Eighty-sixth Street west of Third Avenue. I believe this theatre is still running, and on that bill I was next to closing. I was the eleventh act on the bill, and that pleased me greatly. I stood there watching the show go down. I had written a vaudeville sketch with Lee Randall, and my sister, Katherine Hunter, was working with me. She played the part of Senorita the Dancing Girl. The act was known as *Hunter, Randall and Senorita on the Border of Mexico.* A comedy act. A show stopper. My sister always had to do an encore on her dancing.

So, I watched the other acts, then before we went on, I went up to the dressing room and spoke to my sister:

"If you ever danced in your life, dance tonight."

I turned to my partner and said: "There's a lot of

comedy on this bill. Don't drag nothing. You know I work fast. Keep it moving, feed me fast, keep it moving. Don't give 'em time to think."

I went on out there and broke up the show. They're applauding yet.

When I came off the stage two men approached me in the lobby—a Mr. Howard and Mr. Klause. Mr. Howard said: "I'm a booking agent. I don't want to take you from anybody. If you are signed up with somebody, I'll wait until your contract expires."

I said: "I am not signed up with anybody."

He said: "Can you see me in my office tomorrow?"

I said: "I'll be there."

Well, Howard and Klause signed me up with my vaudeville sketch *On the Border of Mexico*. They signed me to work for two years straight and I got money. I didn't hear any more of that If-you-were-white-the-money-I-could-get-for-you stuff. I worked and got money. It went on for two years, so I worked throughout 1920 and 1922, then I stopped because I did my writing at night. Instead of running around town after my theatre engagement, I would go home to the hotel and write through the night. Now this was when I was writing the musical comedy that turned out to be *How Come?*

At the age of thirty-five, I opened at the Apollo Theatre, Forty-second Street west of Broadway, with my show *How Come?*

The Apollo Theatre referred to by Mr. Hunter is not to be confused with the 125th Street Apollo, which is located in the Harlem area. The Apollo Theatre on Forty-second Street was a popular legitimate theatre which housed such shows as George White's *Scandals*.

The theatre later became known for the showing of foreign films.

It was a success, but it only stayed there for one week due to bad management.

We had a gentleman backing the show—I don't remember his name, let's call him Mr. X—that I liked. While we were out of town with the show, I began to wonder if the managers weren't robbing him. But, my energies were going into the show, and I didn't really do any deep thinking about it. Yet, somehow I was bothered.

What happened was this: Out of town the managers would come to me and say, "Mr. X is coming to town. We told him you paid the salaries for the show." Then, when Mr. X did get into town, he would visit my dressing room and thank me for doing him a favor. I would ask: "What favor?"

And he would answer: "You know, paying the cast salaries."

Then, he would make out a check, give it to me and that check would go right to the managers.

Before the show opened in New York City, I made an appointment to see Mr. X and I met with him and with our lawyers. I related to him some of what I had noticed and he thought about it for a while, then stated:

"I'm going to close the show."

I said: "Now, wait a minute! Why would you close the show? I didn't rob you. My people didn't rob you. I had to keep my mouth shut. I was six months getting this show to Broadway. You know that we would play Washington two or three weeks, then we go on to Philadelphia, then Washington would call us back, and that went on over and over again for six months. I am tired of that. I want to get to Broadway."

So Mr. X put up the money to open at the Apollo on West Forty-second Street. After the money was put up, the managers that were handling the show said: "Now we got him!" They said: "We're going into rehearsal at Vine Hall on Sixth Avenue in New York."

I said: "What're we going into rehearsal for?"

The manager said: "We're going to kick the score out. We're not opening with that score. There are no hit numbers in there."

So, there was nothing I could do about it. Mr. X came to me and said: "Do you see what they're doing to me?"

I said: "I'm very sorry."

They kicked the score out and they brought in Tim Brim, Chris Smith and another party I can't remember now, a dance instructor. As fast as they could they would write the numbers, the company was there in the hall. They would bring up the numbers, play the music, and find new steps and the people would learn the steps. After we did that for a week, we opened at the Apollo.

Soon I told Mr. X the whole story of what had been going on, how I hadn't paid salaries with the checks he gave me, and how the stage manager was walking around with thousand-dollar bills in his pockets. I thought this was a shame and I told him so. He closed the show.

I told him: "While you are fighting those managers in court, take away the shares you gave them. Find a new manager and put me up at the Lafayette Theatre in Harlem, 132nd Street and Seventh Avenue. We'll make money for you while you're fighting in court."

We stayed there for two weeks. We did a jam-up business. After the case was settled in court, we went on the road. That was fine! Three weeks on the road and a notice was put up on the call board stating: "Salaries will be cut."

The backer wanted his money back fast. The company all signed a list: "I Object!" George Cooper— who was once the partner of dancer Bill "Bojangles" Robinson—was my straight man. He signed. Then, I looked and everybody had signed. I said: "I can't do the show by myself."

So I signed.

The stage manager told me: "You know, I had to buy a lot of tickets to get this scenery back to New York, so tell your people I'll sell the tickets half price so they can get their fares back to New York."

I said: "You know my people like I know them. They're not going to buy any tickets from you. I have half of them booked in Chicago already, in night clubs. I am going to keep my cast together."

Very few of them came back to New York. I placed them in jobs. Finally, when I got back to New York, Mr. X phoned me and asked me to come over to Newark, N.J., and talk with him. I did and he said:

"Eddie, we would still be friends if you hadn't signed that list."

I said: "What could I do? I couldn't do the show by myself. I was the last one to sign."

He said: "Yes, but you went to the other side of the fence. You and I could have carried on with this show in another form. We are through."

So, I left.

I never sold or gave away any of my copyrights. But, I signed an option with Mr. X that he could use my sketches or plays up to a certain date. Later on I had bookings at Loew's theatres. One of the main scenes out of *How Come?* was the "Bootleg" scene. I used it during my bookings at this time. It was Prohibition and the scene was a smash. This was the scene where we were on stage making liquor and officers appeared. We talked the officers into not looking while other characters removed the liquor.

Anyway, a week before the option with Mr. X expired, I tried to use my "Bootleg" scene in Newark, and I was stopped by Mr. X. I was forced to stop activities until the option expired.

A note should be made here for younger readers. What happened to Mr. Hunter in relationship to Mr. X and his managers would happen in another way today—such as payroll padding, getting kickbacks from rental of equipment and other practices that border on the illegal. In Mr. Hunter's time Actors' Equity was not the powerful union it is today nor were there iron-clad contracts with other theatrical unions that serve in watchdog capacities to prevent such eager professionals from being used and abused by crooked managers. It is interesting to note that these same unions are constantly blamed for such matters as the high price of tickets and high theatrical costs, yet in truth they have prevented performers from being stranded on the road by demanding the posting of bonds, and by demanding other protective measures. These unions, with all their faults, unjustly remain the "whipping boys" for the exploiters.

Then, in the late 1920's I was working vaudeville at the Loew's American Theatre on Forty-second Street when

I had an offer to go to England with Lew Leslie's *Blackbirds*—to appear in the show and do some writing.

My lawyer drew up a contract stating that my fare to England would be paid. If after three weeks things didn't seem to be working out, my fare home would be paid.

I accepted the offer.

Lew Leslie was the producer of many versions of the show *Blackbirds*. These shows were generally tried out in Harlem night spots, then moved to Broadway. One of Mr. Leslie's foremost stars was the great Florence Mills, who sang her famous song, "I'm a Little Blackbird Looking for a Bluebird," in one of his shows. Miss Mills died in 1927 of a delayed appendix condition. It is said the lyricist Andy Razaf and composer Eubie Blake wrote the hit song "Memories of You" as a tribute to her.

When I landed in England I had already done some writing for the show, and we went right into rehearsal under the title, *Blackbirds*.

After the opening I said to one of the managers: "The billing doesn't seem right to me. Here we have out in front of the theatre, *Blackbirds*, but the cast is all white. Not that I'm prejudiced, but can't you brown them down or something?"

We laughed, but they browned the people down to look like colored folks and we went on with the show and it was a hit. We went on for that year, and I became famous for creating a saying which for a time was very popular and I became known by it. It happened this way: One night I was performing on stage and I couldn't understand why I wasn't getting any laughs. For three weeks I did the show and—no laughs. I'm standing there on stage, doing the show, feeling bad, and the spotlight is on me and in that spotlight I see a vision of a big ship going back to America, and, unconsciously, I said to myself: "Good gracious!"

After the show the producer ran back to me and said: "Say that again!"

"Say what?" I asked.

He said: "Good gracious!"

I said: "I can't say 'Good gracious!' all through the show."

He said: "Didn't you hear them laugh?"

I told him I didn't hear nothing, that I had seen a big ship going back to America and I was homesick and that was what my mind was on.

What really made the saying of "Good gracious!" such a tremendous laugh was the way I said it: in a deep, mournful, weeping voice.

That night also, I said:

"These are your people. What is the matter with them? They don't laugh."

The producer said: "They love you."

"Why don't they make me know it?" I asked. "I'm used to hearing applause."

Here was his explanation: "Suppose you're driving an automobile. You're going sixty miles an hour. Drive thirty."

And he walked out of the dressing room. I asked my partner: "Do you get that?"

He said: "You're too fast."

I said: "All right, let's see if it works out that way. We do two shows a night. Now, the first show we'll play thirty miles an hour and we'll play sixty miles an hour at the second show."

That turned out to be the sinker. I slowed down and they were getting me. I was too fast for them. Now the way I do, if I can get away with being fast, I do it. When I hit Dublin, Ireland, they're just like our folks. They laughed and laughed. Those people are great people. But, finally I got homesick and I said: "I'll go home."

Now, a funny thing happened over there. I ran into a lot of prejudice. You see, over there when you are a comedian in England, you are a star. You live up to that and they respect you as such. I had the best of everything. The average performer over there has a room, a combined room it's called. I had a sleeping room and parlor where you can serve drinks.

I came home from the theatre and the landlady said: "Mr. Hunter, there is a gentleman here from New York who wants to see you."

This was a white gentleman. He said: "You don't know me. I saw the show and I enjoyed it very much. I guess you find a great difference here in England. You take back home in the States, it would be a little different, wouldn't it?"

He went on making a few remarks. I interrupted and said to the landlady: "You know what this gentleman is trying to tell you? If I was in New York, I wouldn't be living in a place like your home. Here I have the best of everything and he sees that and he's prejudiced. Please see him to the door and never mind the drinks."

Another time I was in Edinburgh. I was invited to a dance at the King's Hall. I was on the floor, dancing with the prima donna of the show, white Anita Edwards. The band stopped and we stood there, applauding, waiting for more music to dance to. Across the floor came three southern sailors from an American ship. They came and tried to part me and this white girl.

She said: "Just a minute. I'm dancing with this gentleman."

The dance hall owner came over and said: "Listen, this is Scotland, not America where you do what you want to do."

They rushed those three southern sailors out of there and the whole bunch got in behind them, booting them out. They called me "The Fighting Comedian," but it wasn't that I would fight, but I would fight for my rights. I had built a reputation as a star. If my billing wasn't right when I arrived at the theatre, I would diplomatically call the theatre manager. I would say that my name had to be up there. If he wasn't going to put the name up there, I would take down the scenery and go on to the next town. He would change it. I worked hard to get to that and I fought for that.

Once in vaudeville I went to a town out West. The train was late, so we didn't pull in until two in the morning. There was a white gentleman in the railroad office and he said:

"Well, I'm glad you got in here. Now I'll close up. I'm the manager of this railroad station and I'm the constable of this town."

He was everything in the town. He said: "Now, I'll take you boys to your lodgings."

With us was one white performer, so we walked down to this house in the snow and rang the bell. A white gentleman stuck his head out the window and the constable said: "I've got some performers down here for you to put up."

The man said: "I'll be right down." Then, he stuck his head back out the window and said: "Two is colored and one is white. I'll take the white."

The white fellow with us said: "You can't take them, you can't take me."

I said: "Wait a minute. I don't want you to suffer on my account. You go on. This is a bitter night."

The white performer said: "No, I'm with you."

The owner of the place said: "I'll tell you what you should do. Walk on down the tracks and find an empty car. That'll be better than staying out in this cold."

So, we went on down there and my partner went further down the tracks and found the place where they switch the trains. It was so warm down there that he never came back to tell me what he had found. Me and the white fellow took our overcoats and turned the seats around and made bunks. I found an old lantern and I lit it and put it under the coats. When we woke up, he was looking at me and laughing. He said:

"You're all made up to go on the stage."

The smut from the lantern had blacked my face. I told him his face was black, too. Anyway, we waited until the theatre opened and then I went to the manager and said:

"Before I rehearse I want to know if there is a place where a colored performer can get some lodging."

"No," he said. "But I will have a bed placed in your dressing room and make everything comfortable for you." I refused the offer:

"Well, then, I'm not good enough to play in your town," I said. "I don't perform before people like that."

And I didn't perform.

Sometimes when I was going into a town to perform, I would write the stage manager: "I'm coming into the theatre next week and here are my props: I want a telephone, not one that falls apart. I don't want the phone making my laughs. A living room couch, not one that's falling apart. I need a bed for my bedroom scene, not one you get in and the slats give away. I'll write my own laughs."

So, I'd arrive a couple of days earlier and check out the props. If something wasn't working, then I'd say: "I don't want that." That's where I got the name as a "Fighting Comedian." Some people don't know how to talk up for themselves. I remember working at the 125th Street Apollo and poor Sandy Burns—he's dead now—was playing on the bill with me. He wanted a chicken coop built. They gave him an old big carton that they'd taken a radio out of or something and made that into a chicken coop. When Sandy tried to crawl in to get the chickens, the coop was moving all over the stage and people were laughing in the wrong places."

The manager said: "Hey, Hunter, have you got another sketch you can put in? I'm going to let Sandy out."

I said: "No, you don't. You're at fault here. He wanted a crate for chickens and you gave him a cardboard box. When he tries to get in through the opening, it's going all over the stage. That's not his fault. Let the man downstairs build him a crate and I'm sure you will find a difference."

They built him a crate and the second show went on. Had I agreed with the manager, Sandy would have been out of a job. I was always for the right. Now, that's my story in show business . . .

But, I do want to mention my favorite comedians besides Sandy Burns. There were Apus Brooks, Billy Higgins, Andrew Trevell, Alex Lovejoy, Pigmeat

Markham, Eddie Green, Johnny Lee Long—and here I ought to stop because there were some great ones, some real great ones. There was Joe Byrd, Sandy Burns' friend. I worked in a sketch in Philadelphia where I had the opening on the bill and Sandy closed. He got good laughs.

The old Standard Theatre was on South Street in Philadelphia. Dick Campbell will tell you the manager, Mr. Gibson, was tight with money. He was always trying to pull me down. I said: "Wait a minute! I don't live in Philadelphia. You can't pay me *that* kind of money." And I'd always win. He treated me like a gentleman, but I had to fight.

You would have to resort to some unusual activities in order to create the pressure to get what you wanted. The late Richard B. Harrison said: "A lot of times they'd promise you $500, then cut the ciphers off."

Another thing I want to mention is the Theatrical Owners and Bookers Association that used to book black actors from coast to coast. A performer could be booked for fifty-two weeks out of the year. He knew where he was going to be each and every week and his mail could be forwarded right on to him. We called the outfit Toby-time.

Toby-time or the Toby circuit was the nickname for the organization known as Theatrical Owners and Bookers Association. It was also jokingly and affectionately known as "Tough on Black Actors."

In *Black Drama* I wrote: "This organization booked Negro performers into houses across the nation. It must be remembered that around the turn of the twentieth century there were about five thousand theatres in the United States. Almost every city boasted one or more resident companies and these theatres attracted great stars from the New York stage. The arrival of talking pictures brought a decline in the number of these theatres and by 1940 there remained only about two hundred professional theatres in the entire country. But these theatres were there in the days of Toby-time and veteran actor George Wiltshire declared once that endless work made it possible for actors to constantly polish their techniques. The rise of the movie medium and the growing influence of white managers destroyed Toby-time. But, Toby-time left us many fine veterans and they paved the way for others."

Sidney Easton said that black performers didn't know what it was to be unemployed as long as Toby-time existed. It was really a training ground for a lot of performers who came on in later years. I found that people who had that kind of theatre background got to play Broadway shows, they excelled because they had developed through constant exposure and they had refined their talent to the point where it was natural. One particular person was Ethel Waters.

You see, they played before people who had absolutely no qualms whatsoever about letting you know if they didn't like what you were doing.

Now, you know I want to talk about the Crescent. That was the first black theatre organized in the Harlem area, right there on 135th Street. That was the main street then. Everything was there. The nightclubs. Everything. Where the Crescent was is now the Lenox Apartments.

I put on stock there. Three weeks. Four weeks. Six weeks. Then, I kind of got tired and I begged out for a rest. I went down to Asbury Park and stopped at the Whitman Sisters' home to get some rest. I wasn't there any time before a telegram came, saying: "Come on back. They want you." So, I had to come on back to the Crescent. In the meantime, the Lincoln Theatre—that one's now a church—put on stock to run against me. But I was making money for them. The crowd waiting to see me went from the Crescent down past the Lincoln and around the corner. When they were waiting to see me, some would drop off into the Lincoln. We were going fast, cutting out pictures. We were doing seven and eight shows a day.

Once a discussion came up about black comedians putting burnt cork on their faces. I said: "Let me tell you something: I don't need cork to be funny. It is just what they are doing these days, so I put it on. For instance, if you play Boston, on Sunday you can't put on any cork up there. You walk on just as you come in off the street, do your act, and then go on about your business. That proves it to me. I got my laughs."

A bet came up about that and I said I'd do a sketch in which I wouldn't use cork. I decided to write a sketch called *The Gentleman Burglar* and do it straight faced in my cutaway tails, high silk hat and to come on in class. A gentleman burglar, and I'd bring this girl on as my lady friend. I'd come in my evening clothes and she was in her evening gown. I'd say:

"How do you like it, honey?"

She'd say: "Oh, it's a marvelous place."

I'd say: "Look around. Make yourself at home."

The audience would think: Here's a guy bringing a lady in the house. You know what I mean. But, she was working with me in this racket. She'd say:

"That's a beautiful boudoir."

I'd say: "Go in and rest yourself."

I'd walk into the chamber and act just like the guy who owned the place. I'd go over and fix myself a drink and then I'd put on my gloves and say: "Now, to get to work."

I would go over to a safe by the window and just as I would start to turn it, Billy Higgins—my favorite comedian—would raise the window up, throw the bag in noisily, and I'd run behind the coat tree and have my gun right on him. He'd come in with a hammer and a tool and he'd break the safe open. After he'd get it open, I'd step forward and say:

"Thanks. You saved me a whole lot of trouble."

He'd say: "Please don't call the cops. Don't have me locked up."

I'd say: "If you want to be in this racket, why don't you make it legitimate? It is guys like you that are making it hard for me! Sit down!"

He'd say: "I'm not tired."

I have the gun on him and I'd say: "Sit down!!!" And on that he'd say: "Yes, sir."

I'd say: "Now, pick up that jewel and hand it here." I would put on the glass and examine the jewel he gave me. I would examine one diamond, then another and then I'd say: "I'll take this one. You can have that one. That's good enough for a rat like you." Then, I'd give him another and I'd say: "Here, take this and buy yourself some cheese."

He'd say: "But, a rat don't eat cheese *all* the time!"

I'd take all the good stuff and give him the junk, then I'd say: "I'll tell you what you do: If anyone comes, you hide under that table and when I say 'Go', you beat it out that window as fast as you can."

A knock at the door! An officer appears and asks: "Do you live here?"

I'd say: "Yes, officer. What's wrong?"

He'd say: "As I was coming down the street, I saw a character going up the fire escape. I don't know what apartment he went in."

I'd say: "Well, me and my wife just came in from a nightclub a few minutes ago. Everything seems to be in order here. I'll tell you what you do: You go upstairs and look around and in the meantime I'll investigate the other rooms."

He'd say: "All right."

So, he's going upstairs and while he's gone the real tenant comes in. He is jumping around! I say: "Shhh! Don't get excited. I'm a detective incognito. I saw a character coming up the fire escape, but I don't know which apartment he went in. I checked that room, so you go in that room over there. Here, take this gun and don't come out until I say 'go.'" And remember, Higgins is under the table and he'd hear me say "Go" and he'd go! I'd hear the policeman coming and I'd start yelling: "Help! Police!" and then I'd shout "Go" and the real tenant would come out of the room with the gun and I'd say to the policeman: "There's your man." The policeman would take him away and I'd put on my top hat, wink at the audience and walk out. It was a scream.

All of this was without burnt cork. And it worked!

As I said before, you couldn't wear burnt cork in Boston because of the Sunday Law. No costumes or anything. Not on Sunday. You could just walk in off the street. Just like Philadelphia has that law about no liquor on Sunday. No Sunday shows. It was like that then. I don't know how it is now in Philadelphia. But, when you were playing Boston in those days they would tell you right away: No costumes. No makeup on Sunday. So, you'd be out—maybe at a party—and then you'd have to get on down to the theatre and do your part. You'd just walk in and do what you had to do and go on about your business. Cork didn't mean anything and I proved it to them, just like I proved it in *The Gentleman Burglar*.

Mr. Hunter is too modest to mention here that his gentleman burglar assisted in the development of a long line of thieves of this nature—Ronald Colman in *Raffles,* Edmund Lowe in numerous films, and Cesar Romero and Clive Brook to mention a few.

Oh, there were a lot of things I went through! Did you ever run into prejudice in your business? Funny thing. I'm in a Western town. The manager hollers: "Mr. Hunter, come on down here. There's someone who wants to see you."

So I come on down and there are two gentlemen there. I didn't even have time to remove the cork from my face. I'm still in costume with my white gloves on. When I walked up to them, one man said:

"My friend and I were betting that you were a white man under cork."

I pulled the gloves off and said: "You lose."

He said: "But you don't use 'dis here' and 'dat' and 'dem.' You talk. How do you do that? You do comedy and get across and you don't talk like a colored man. How do you do that?"

I said: "Well, does a colored man have a special way to talk?"

He said: "This is strange. I don't know how I lost."

I said: "Well, I'll tell you gentlemen: This is a funny thing. I'm of a mixed marriage. Maybe I get it from that. My mother is white and my father is colored."

Conversation ended. That left them cold.

I said to myself: "That's funny. Every time I say that the conversation ends. I know! I'm going to try it another way." So, the next time someone came up with that, I said: "My father was white and my mother was colored," and the conversation would go on. But, the minute I'd say my mother was white—Bing! I'd done something to them.

That stopped them dead. No more fun.

Yeah, I thought I'd try it the other way. My father was colored and when I said that the conversation ended. I thought: "What a difference it makes!" But today it's different. It's not that way now. But, it was an uphill battle all the way. I had to fight. It was tough, but I took those blows amazingly good. I said: "Someday my day'll come around and I'll demand the respect I'm due." And I got it.

Now, about my shining hour—or hours. Well, the Crescent Theatre was certainly a great one. By 1909 show business for us was slowing down in white theatres. The Crescent kept calling on me. I had plenty of written material—so much that sometimes I would change acts twice a week. The public would demand revivals of our sketches and we would bring them back—*What Happens When the Husbands Leave Home, The Railroad Porter,* and *Subway Sal* were among our hits. Sometimes, while all of this was going on, I would remember that agent who told me: "If you were white, the money I could get for you!"

Then, I would smile and remember those booking

agents—Howard and Klause—who took me over. And we made money.

Then, among those shining hours is the trip to England. I had been under the care of Dr. Louis T. Wright. He said I had bad lungs and he advised against the trip. Well, I went anyway and a doctor over there told me I had to drink lots of liquor. I didn't drink liquor, but I decided to try. I drank hot Scotch. I drank hot Scotch and I made it to this age.

Another great thing that happened to me was in 1968 when the people of Harlem gave me a salute for contributing to the Black Theatre movement. The *Amsterdam News* carried a story about it and the people behind the whole thing—Randolph A. Rankin and Madolyn Conley—brought Dick Campbell, Loften Mitchell, Horace Carter and Frank Gaskin Fields, the musician, to my house. They presented me with a plaque that hangs from my wall right now, framed. I felt great, great! Yes, I really felt great knowing that people appreciated the things I had done and remembered me.

That plaque and other awards of honor—they are all there in my home. When I pass away, maybe I'll turn it all over to my friend, artist Earl Sweeting. Sometimes I take out all of those things and look at them— at the stuff I did when I started off. Sometimes I say: "Did I write this?" Terrible how a man can improve! But, when I think about this, something inside says to me: "Don't throw that stuff away! Keep it to show how a man struggles to get to a point!"

Yes, it's been a struggle, but it's all gratifying when you realize people have appreciated you and now they are calling you a pioneer when you never thought you were doing a thing but struggling. But, the whole thing makes me happy about something I told agent Marty Falkins after I retired from the theatre. Marty handled Bill "Bojangles" Robinson and he spoke to me about a television engagement. I told Marty:

"I don't want to be bothered. I'll stand on my record. Let the people who know me remember me at my best. I don't want to go back now and have people see me when I'm older and when I can't put on the speed I had. I've got sense enough to know that I can't do what I used to do. If I get to talking too much, I get winded. Folks will ask: 'What's the matter with him? He ain't like he used to be.'"

I also told Marty that I was going to let people remember me at the top. I told him that I thought that was the trouble with a lot of prizefighters: They retire, then they retire from their retirement and get back in the ring and someone else *retires* them. They are knocked out. Beaten. I didn't want anything like that. I retired myself.

And I sipped my hot Scotch. Dick Campbell once asked me if I attribute my longevity to hot Scotch. I wouldn't exactly claim *that*, but I would say that it has helped me to enjoy my longevity.

Regina M. Andrews

A Voice: Regina M. Andrews

Long before I met Regina M. Andrews I knew many lovely things about her. And I also knew of her husband, former State Assemblyman William T. Andrews. They had long been in the forefront of the civic, cultural and political struggles in Harlem.

The way I met her amuses me to this very day. I graduated from high school at seventeen and, not having the money to get into college, I decided to involve myself in the professional theatre. Although I did some acting, I was primarily interested in learning all that I could about the theatre. And I belonged to several Harlem groups, notably John Bunn's Progressive Dramatizers at Salem Methodist Church, the Pioneer Drama Group and the Rose McClendon Players, organized by Dick Campbell and his late wife, Muriel Rahn.

That is what led me to Regina M. Andrews' doorstep. I was writing plays every time anyone could look twice. And I hope those plays are all lost. I was taking Dick Campbell a play each and every week the Good Lord sent. Now, it was all Dick could do to finance five plays a year. Finally, he had a discussion with Jean Blackwell Hutson, now the curator of the Schomburg Center in Harlem. And Dick called me in to see him. He said:

"Young man, Regina Andrews is the chief librarian down at the 115th Street Library. There is a theatre in the library basement. Why don't you and your friends go down there and organize a theatre and put on your plays?"

I said, naively:

"Mr. Campbell, you taught us to be team players. Won't it be disloyal for me to go down there. I mean—won't it make you mad?"

His answer was classic:

"Young man, you have no idea how happy you would make me by going down there."

That is exactly how I got down to the 115th Street Library and met the beautiful Regina M. Andrews. I see her right now with a lovely smile on a reddish brown face, framed by black hair with a trace of gray. Her clothing was immaculate, lovely without being ostentatious. Her gentle voice flowed with tenderness. And when she walked images of African queens filled my mind, but she did not flaunt it or speak to you in a condescending manner.

Me? I was nervous. I stood there, fidgeting nervously, knowing well that I was in the presence of a great human being. I was awed. And I looked at my ragged clothing and I was embarrassed over the manner of my dress. No one ever gave me an award for being the Best Dressed Man any place, any time. This was always a source of embarrassment to my family and my friends, who particularly disliked my hats. And I am certain that it is still a source of embarrassment. Ordinarily, I do not care, but in the presence of Regina M. Andrews I did care.

She did not even mention her own theatrical career, but I knew and I kept waiting to talk about it. She had, along with Harold Jackman, Dorothy Peterson and others, organized the Harlem Experimental Theatre. This group functioned at St. Philip's Episcopal Church on West 134th Street, where the late Sheldon Hale Bishop was the rector. This is the same church where Dr. M. Moran Weston is now the rector and the same church where actor Al Fann has done so well with his play *King Heroin*.

Regina M. Andrews wrote many of the plays produced by the Harlem Experimental Theatre. I had read the rave reviews about her work, and I think it is an indication of her character that she wrote under an assumed name and remained in the background, modestly. And many, many people told me of the way she blushed when a newspaper reporter broke the story and told all of Harlem that Regina M. Andrews was the real name of the highly acclaimed playwright. Significantly, I do not remember the *nom de plume*, but I do remember Regina M. Andrews. And I also knew that she had been actively interested in the Krigwa Players, a group founded by the late Dr. W. E. B. DuBois to preserve the black folk play. I knew she knew playwright Eulalie Spence, who had won an award for her work.

Oh, there were a thousand questions I wanted to ask her, but I sat fidgeting and listening.

Yes, she said, we youngsters could use the theatre any night we wanted to use it. Rehearsal space was given to us free of charge, but on production nights we would have to stay a little later to clean up and pay the custodian's fee of two dollars for the night.

Man!

We youngsters went roaring into that library basement. We raised hell! Cats had never seen a lighting board before and we had to try that out. Eugene Coates was the stage manager, but he had to push the actors away from his lighting board. And what we put on there for our first show would have gotten us put out of any other theatre. We called ourselves the Pioneer Drama Group and our acting company for our first play there included Beatrice Albertus, Willard Bartley, Richard Fisher, Clayton Mitchell, Charles Isaacs and Louis Mitchell.

I had written two one-acters: *Cocktails* and *Cross Roads*. *Cocktails* had music by Catherine Richardson and it told the ridiculous story of Father Divine running for president. He promised to give out canned chicken instead of relief beef and he was swept into office. There he presided in the Black House and he promptly got himself into trouble. The big munitions makers wanted him to declare war, but Father Divine had planned to use the Navy's battleships for his yacht parties. He also had his troubles with the Supreme Court for he kept beating the justices at the dice table. The Father was deposed from the presidency and the black columnist, Walter Wenchmore, who had exposed him, was the man who replaced him. Even when a black man wins, he loses.

The second play, *Cross Roads*, dealt with the Harlem riot of 1935, led by a young man who was encouraged by a former slave. We had one scene where black men tried to lynch a white man to a lamp post on 125th Street. Naturally, our hero was framed for murder and sent to the electric chair. But, the play ended with the black people regrouping, getting ready for a real riot that would bring total freedom.

I told you we were crazy then. But, Mrs. Andrews didn't think so. She attended opening night and she got up and urged the audience members to go out and get more audiences. And so we kept on putting on those two plays. Someone went down to the Public Library headquarters and complained to Mrs. Andrews' bosses about the work we were doing. I was standing there in her office when she told the downtown bosses to go to hell.

I was shocked. I forgot that kind, gentle people can get mad. But I soon learned that Mrs. Andrews could really tell people off in direct terms. For example: The custodian of the library saw that we were drawing good houses and since we were only teen-agers he thought he could pull a fast one. He not only wanted the two dollars we paid him nightly, but two dollars more.

What I heard Mrs. Andrews tell that man cannot be put in print. I do not want to embarrass her. Let me simply state that we continued to pay two dollars per night for performances.

We remained at the 115th Street Library until 1939, after which I went away to college, then the Navy, then graduate school. By 1946 we were back at the 115th Street Library, calling ourselves the 115th Street People's Theatre. We produced seven plays before the end of 1948, including the first versions of my plays, *The Cellar* and *The Bancroft Dynasty.*

We left and Mrs. Andrews objected strenuously. But, someone had gone downtown on us again and this time the library system came down on our heads. No tickets could be sold. Period. We could not produce plays without earning money and so we all cried and we left our home on 115th Street. We went out into the world and formed the Harlem Showcase.

Soon after, Mrs. Andrews left the library and I have not since walked by that building despite the fact that my family home is only two blocks away. And any time I go into a library I see the face of Regina M. Andrews.

I have been fortunate enough to see her on numerous times—at Frank's over lunch, at the *Harlem on My Mind* affair at the Metropolitan Museum. She spearheaded that affair and moderated a session in memory of the late Langston Hughes. Later, too, Dick Campbell and I taped a television show on the Black Theatre for NBC and we did this in her living room on Edge-combe Avenue.

Now she has stepped forward again to tell you about the Krigwa Players and the Harlem Experimental Theatre.

To get back to that black man in the restaurant, I took a long time trying to get you ready for her. And here she is:

THE WORDS OF

Regina M. Andrews

Before going into the personal side of the early little theatre in Harlem, I want to mention and give tribute to those who preceded us with their courage and conviction and belief that the Negro creative artist had a contribution to make to the culture of America. This goes back prior to 1920; to men like James Weldon Johnson, who encouraged the Harlem Renaissance writer. Johnson wrote two books of Negro spirituals before we were even thinking about doing creative dramas for popular production. Johnson was a black Broadway pioneer, and he produced songs and plays with his brother, J. Rosamond Johnson, and Bob Cole. James Weldon Johnson wrote the lyrics and J. Rosamond Johnson the music for the song "Lift Every Voice and Sing," which came to be known as the Negro national anthem.

Then there was James P. Johnson, one of the outstanding pianist-composers, who played the rags of Scott Joplin. We can't forget these creative artists because they are a part of our cultural history.

Eric Walrond from British Guiana was another whom we encouraged, and who in turn encouraged us. I think it's important that we recognize the contributions of West Indian Americans to our American culture. I could recall many, many names of these early settlers who came of their own volition to the United States and settled in the New York area.

There was the lyricist Andy Razaf, for instance. Andy died recently; however, you knew him as the grandson of a king in Madagascar; but you know him also because of "Honeysuckle Rose," "Memories of You," and "You and Your Luck to Me."

Tribute should also be paid to Marcus Garvey because I feel very strongly that this man started the first mass determination movement in Harlem. We will remember the leadership of this great Jamaican.

William H. Ferris wrote an early book, *The African Abroad* (1913), which could today be a reference book in any school. And surely we want to mention Dr. William Edward Burghardt DuBois, whose influence and encouragement eased the growing pains of the Harlem Experimental Theatre. Many Americans learned to know another side of Dr. DuBois when he wrote *The Litany of Atlanta* after the rioting in that city in 1906.

We also had our early soapbox orators who had no place to go except to street corners. There was Hubert Harrison from St. Croix, George Schuyler the satirist from Syracuse, and A. Philip Randolph, another of our early soapbox orators. Mr. Randolph edited *The Messenger*, and within its covers many of our early poets, writers and dramatists saw their works published.

Men of courage of the period included Roy Lancaster, Chandler Owen, assistant editor of *The Messenger*, fiction-writer Wallace Thurman, Cyril D. Briggs from the Dutch West Indies, and Richard B. Moore, one of the first bookshop owners in Harlem. George Young had preceded him with a bookshop on 135th Street. Mr. Moore's resourceful shop was on 125th Street where the new State Office Building now stands.

And there was Joel A. Rogers, the early historian. Commentaries on his writing have been appearing in newspapers of late. Rogers wrote *From Superman to Man* and other highly intellectual books. There was W. A. Domingo from Jamaica who edited *Challenge*.

These remarks serve as an introduction to our years with the Harlem Experimental Theatre beginning in 1927. By this time we had the confidence of men who had achieved a great deal before us. But, somewhere along the line a few of us sat in the basement of the 135th Street Library one night, and we began to talk about wanting to write and produce our own dramas. Plays and revues of black people were on downtown stages, but few were presented in Harlem where the black playwright's audience lived. We had few plays to work with and almost none of recent date.

We wanted the Harlem Experimental Theatre to be patterned on the plan of the Krigwa Theatre. Here something must be said about Krigwa because that was our parent dramatic group in New York City.

Krigwa. From where did the name come? It came from the *Crisis* Guild of Writers and Artists (Crigwa) —Dr. DuBois' original gathering of writers and artists. The group name was spelled with a "C" at that time, but within a short time it was changed to Krigwa.

Crisis Magazine, as you know, is the official publication of the National Association for the Advancement of Colored People. As of this writing the magazine is edited by Henry Lee Moon, author of *The Emerging Thought of W. E. B. DuBois*. Dr. DuBois, one of the founders of the NAACP, now lies in his grave in Ghana. Mr. Moon publishes in each issue a statement from Dr. DuBois written many years ago. These statements

are applicable to conditions in many parts of the
United States today.

About 1924—perhaps in August—*Crisis Magazine*
had its annual contest, and people began contributing
manuscripts for prizes known as the Amy Spingarn
Awards. I wish everyone could have known Joel, Amy,
and Arthur Spingarn. Amy Spingarn felt that if black
writers could be encouraged, the world would have
historic material. Therefore, achievement prizes were
named for her. In the year 1924, there were 628 manuscripts submitted from all across the country. Among
those submitted came the manuscript for the play
called *Black Man of Fantasy* by Charles Burroughs.
There were several other excellent scripts which were
later produced.

Dr. DuBois at this time established the Krigwa
Theatre. His philosophy was: The Negro Art Theatre
should be (1) a theatre about us, (2) a theatre by us,
(3) a theatre for us and (4) a theatre near us. So
Krigwa was established right in our own community,
and our writers began to produce their first plays in
Harlem.

Two books should be mentioned at this point: *The
New Negro* (1925) by Alain Locke gave an erudite
and wonderful picture of this period; and *Plays and
Pageants of Negro Life* (1930) by Willis Richardson,
which contains excellent examples of these "early
plays."

Dr. Alain Locke, a Rhodes scholar and later a professor
at Howard University, was one of the great promoters
of the black artistic movement. Willis Richardson was
by anyone's standards a splendid playwright.

It is important to note here that Mrs. Andrews' and Dr. DuBois' definition of theatre differs from Eddie Hunter's definition. To put it in simplistic terms—and to possibly oversimplify matters—Mrs. Andrews and Dr. DuBois were talking in terms of serious drama in the manner of Ibsen, Chekhov, O'Casey and other playwrights. Mr. Hunter was a showman, a musical comedy man.

This was the age of the musical comedy, the Cinderella type theatre, and it permeated white and black theatre. But a very important thing was happening. The Abbey Theatre in Ireland had turned its back upon European theatre and dedicated itself to the writing and producing of indigenous Irish drama. The white American theatre at the time turned its back on European drama and Eugene O'Neill, Sidney Howard, Philip Barry and S. N. Behrman—to mention a few—wrote out of the American white experience. Plays no longer had "happy" endings and Sidney Howard's *They Knew What They Wanted* utilized what critics like Joseph Wood Krutch and John Gassner called "The New Morality." Mr. Howard dealt with a woman who had an out-of-wedlock child by her husband's friend—and the husband accepted this child because he knew what he wanted and that was a family.

Mrs. Andrews, Dr. DuBois and others sought the same type of revolutionary theatre in black terms. Hindsight compels one to note that they were raging successes. Had O'Neill, Howard and company not existed, the possibility of Odets, Williams, Miller and others rising in the white theatre might have been virtually impossible. The same is true in black theatre. Without Mrs. Andrews, Dr. DuBois and others there would have been no Langston Hughes, Lorraine Hansberry, William Branch, Alice Childress, Louis Peterson and others during the 1950's and no James Baldwin, Imamu Amiri Baraka (LeRoi Jones), Larry Neal, Ed Bullins, Joseph A. Walker and other brilliant black playwrights during the 1960's and 1970's.

Historical lines are not as blurred as the enemies of history would make them seem. The truths hidden in history have a way of erupting into subway deficits, bombing raids and Watergates as well as in polarization and racism.

Many encouraged the participation of blacks in the so-called Little Theatre Movement in New York and elsewhere: Ellen Donsen, James Butcher, Shirley Graham with her opera *Tom Tom*, and Randolph Edmonds with his *Six Plays for the Negro Theatre*.

In the 1920's Krigwa had its headquarters in the 135th Street Library. Ernestine Rose was the chief librarian there, and she worked beyond the library's scheduled obligations. She welcomed this first theatre group. I have always been very glad that I was on Miss Rose's staff because she gave me a great deal of latitude in planning cooperation with community organizations. Within the library we provided a platform for the soapbox orator. Our small auditorium offered one of the first platforms he had in Harlem.

One of the outstanding successes of the Krigwa group was the prize-winning production of Eulalie Spence's *The Fool's Errand.* Composed to a great extent of members who had to earn a living outside the theatre, the Krigwa suffered the fate of numerous black theatre groups and eventually folded.

When Dorothy Peterson, Harold Jackman, and one or two others sat with me and discussed how we could re-create the little theatre Dr. DuBois had established with Krigwa, we met in the 135th Street Library, not in our apartments.

The apartment I lived in was shared with a friend, Ethel Ray Nance, an assistant to Charles Johnson. Our apartment was a meeting place for many writers and artists in Harlem. However, we began to have our meetings concerned with the theatre at the 135th Street Library. What do we want to do? What is our goal? What are we going to achieve? These were the questions.

And so the Harlem Experimental Theatre was born. I think it important to emphasize our local community support because our dreams could not have come true without local financing and encouragement. We had a wonderful board of advisors, all extremely cooperative; unfortunately, none are alive today. Yet, I cannot forget what financially secure Harlemites and a few downtowners did to make the Harlem Experimental Theatre a reality.

Mrs. Sallie Alexander, Mrs. Corinne Wright, Elmer A. Carter, Mrs. Jessie Fauset Harris, assistant editor of *Crisis Magazine*, Rose McClendon, the noted actress who later became one of our directors, Mrs. Ruth Logan Roberts, daughter of a former treasurer of Tuskegee Institute, Mrs. John E. Nail, the wife of a real estate dealer, Mrs. Hannah Moriarita, a college director, Miss Elizabeth Stuyvesant, another librarian, Dr. W. E. B. DuBois, Dr. Alain Locke, and Mr. Josiah Marble all encouraged us. Our early directors included Helen Brooks, teacher in the dramatic department at

Hunter College, and Robert Dunmore, and Robert Dorsey was our stage designer.

Mr. Charles Johnson, referred to by Mrs. Andrews, was an eminent educator and college president. Jessie Fauset Harris was also a novelist and teacher at DeWitt Clinton High School.

The 135th Street Library! In its basement the Krigwa group worked. Here appeared the Harlem Experimental Theatre. Here, too, came the Harlem Suitcase Theatre with Langston Hughes' *Don't You Want to Be Free?* when it moved from its loft on West 125th Street. And here Abram Hill and Frederick O'Neal brought into being the American Negro Theatre. In this same basement theatre such plays as Mr. Hill's *Striver's Row* and *Walk Hard* were shown. Here Theodore Browne's *Natural Man* had a remarkable run. And here the Negro version of *Anna Lucasta* was first produced. It was this work that later moved to Broadway and enjoyed a long, successful run.

If the walls of the 135th Street Library could write, this book might be unnecessary.

Neither time nor space permits the recording of letters and releases about the Harlem Experimental Theatre. In the beginning we decided we would not limit ourselves to Negro plays until we could produce our own. So, our first production was *The Duchess Says Her Prayers* by Mary Cass Canfield and *The No 'Count Boy* by Paul Green.

Wonderful photographs in my collection include a beautiful picture of guest artist Edna Lewis Thomas, who was not getting Broadway employment at the time because she fell into the bromide that concerns the various complexions of black Americans: "Too white to be black, and too black to be white." There exist also production photos of sociologist Ira De A. Reid, assistant editor of *Opportunity Magazine*, official publication of the National Urban League. Ira was one of our excellent actors. Also, we have production photos of *The No 'Count Boy*, whose author, Paul Green of North Carolina, was established and accepted in the South long before his acceptance in New York. We had in the cast of *The No 'Count Boy* Leontha Wright, Robert Dorsey, James Thibodeaux and Cecil Scott. The play was a great success according to drama critics of the day. Yes, we were encouraged. After several years at the 135th Street Library, we moved to St. Philip's Church Parish House. The Reverend Shelton Hale Bishop, rector, welcomed us with great warmth, and there we produced *Coastwise* by Isadore Bennett; also, *The Prodigal Son* by Harry Camp, *Get Thee Behind Me, Satan* by Robert Dorsey, and *The Little Stone House* by George Cogman. The playwrights mentioned here were some of our original participants. We later produced plays at St. Martin's Episcopal Church, and dance programs at the Harlem Y.M.C.A.

Then we came to a period of new direction. The talented Rose McClendon became a part of our group as a director. Rose was then a Broadway star, and we were very fortunate when she came to St. Philip's and gave professional leadership to the Harlem Experimental Theatre. She encouraged us, and she especially encouraged production of original plays.

To exist we had to raise funds, and we had occasional receptions at the Witoka Club with such honored guests as Dr. DuBois, Mary White Ovington, Dr. and Mrs. M. V. Boutté and Walter White. On one occasion we raised over eight hundred dollars. After this financial success, we undertook a more serious type of drama, including my play *Climbing Jacob's Ladder*, which was the story of a lynching. The lynching took place while people were in a church praying. Many of the cast went from this production to Broadway. I wrote the play *Climbing Jacob's Ladder* under an assumed name, Ursala Trelling, because of my professional association with the library.

The Harlem Experimental Theatre actually served as a creative production center for the playwright, the actor, the costume and stage designer and the director. Besides the plays I've already mentioned, we produced Andrew Burris' *You Must Be Born Again*, Ted Martin's *Eviction*, and Georgia Douglas Johnson's *Plumes*.

Among our designers of original stage sets was Robert Dorsey, a student at the Mechanics Institute of New York City. Dorsey's creative talent veered toward the modernistic. Among our talented directors were J. Percy Bond, Emmett Lampkin, Margaret LeSoeur of the Sargent School of Dramatics, Robert Dunmore, formerly of Chicago, and Helen Brooks of Hunter College. Serafin Alvarez and Joaquin Alvarez Quintero's play, *A Sunny Morning*, was directed by Dorothy Peterson. Writer, drama critic and Broadway playwright Pierre Loving and author Carl Glick, who conducted our playwrighting class, wrote of the talent and promise inherent in our non-professional efforts. Glick had been a former director of The Little Theatre, San Antonio, Texas. There was also John O'Shaughnessy of the Repertory Players, who gave a real boost to our productions.

Among the talented young persons who contributed to the success of the Harlem Experimental Theatre were Ismay Andrews, Charles Alston, Clarence Hargraves, Goldie Whittington, McCleary Stinette, Van Woodward, Eulabelle Moore, Grant Reynolds, Sadie Stocton, Reginald Goodwin, Ruth Lewis and Alta Douglas, wife of artist Aaron Douglas, who at that early point in his career, designed our programs.

Among recognized black leaders and publications encouraging our dramatic talents were A. Philip Randolph and Chandler Owen, *The New York Age*, the *Pittsburgh Courier*, Elmer Carter of *Opportunity Magazine*, the *Afro-American* and the *Chicago Defender*.

Richard B. Harrison, star of *The Green Pastures*, doffed his celestial robes one evening and journeyed to Harlem to see one of our productions. He chose two members of the cast to return with him to be given parts in *The Green Pastures*. The two lucky ones were Dorothy Peterson and Inez Wilson. Dorothy Peterson was our theatre's executive director. I had the honor of replacing her in that role when she went to Broadway.

Rhetoric was not the name of the game when the Harlem Experimental Theatre was recognized as one of the early groups laying the groundwork for the Federal Theatre to come to Harlem. I should add names of other officers of the theatre. Among them, Dorothy Williams, now involved in the work of the United Nations, Gladys S. Reid, Benjamin Locke, Philitus Joyce of the National Urban League, Irene

C. Malvin, Robert T. Elzy of the Brooklyn Urban League and Mrs. Roy Wilkins.

I want to deal for a moment with the play *Climbing Jacob's Ladder*. This was one of my first plays. Before coming to New York, I had been very much influenced by Ida B. Wells Barnett of Chicago. She wrote the first *Red Record*, in which were published the first figures on the number of lynchings in this country. This was submitted to the NAACP, and this among other incidents led Assistant Secretary Walter White to go South and investigate lynchings. When I was a child in Chicago and first heard of lynchings, they were incomprehensible. It's understandable that in my twenties I would have to write a play about lynching. And I did, in the year 1931.

When I took *Climbing Jacob's Ladder* downtown to Dr. DuBois' office, he said:

"Regina, I would like you to come back and have tea with me in about a week, after I have had time to read it."

Oh, this was a wonderful experience—to have tea with Dr. DuBois and possibly hear praise of my first play! The week passed. Everything was very quiet when I entered his reception room—an envelope was in his hand.

We had tea, and talked about many things, and then I thought it was time to go. He said: "Regina, in this envelope is your play. Take it back and write it over and be very careful of what you are doing. You can do better than this, and I urge you to do better. Then, bring it back to me."

Well, this was the jolt that I needed. I had enjoyed writing under an assumed name. I thought this meant success; however, I took the play home and revised my writing.

After production, Dr. DuBois wrote me, saying:

"Dear Regina: I saw your play last night but had to hurry off before getting a chance to speak to you.

"The second play was beautifully done, and the first one not at all bad; but the third, your play, was thrilling. I enjoyed it immensely, and it gripped the audience. Congratulations on it. Sometime we'll talk it over." I was indeed proud of these words of praise from Dr. DuBois!

This note of intrusion is to state that Mrs. Andrews might well be proud of being praised by Dr. DuBois. Dr. DuBois had one of the greatest minds produced on American soil. He was also quite blunt, absolutely honest and forthright and absolutely uncompromising. He constantly sought the truth and it led him to many, many battles.

In fact, Mrs. Andrews showed more courage than this writer. I admired Dr. DuBois, but I kept my distance from him. I was not about to incur his biting tongue. He barred nobody when it came to shouting the truth. Once when the Federal Bureau of Investigation sent agents to the NAACP office, they asked what the NAACP was trying to do. Dr. DuBois snapped at them: "We're trying to make the United States Constitution a reality."

Those agents got out of that building in a hurry!

My Harlem Experimental Theatre scrapbook is filled with many long letters from various drama critics of the era. Despite this praise, we had to go through a period wherein the community wondered if it really needed a theatre. The Harlem Adult Education Committee took this matter in hand on a particular Sunday and discussed it.

The Committee decided that Harlem very definitely needed a theatre and drama. All ethnic groups and peoples need the dramatic forms of cultural expression. Krigwa and our Harlem Experimental Theatre helped to establish this ideal.

I am confident that our work inspired other groups, and may have been the shot in the arm that brought the Federal Theatre (W.P.A.) to New York. I know many of our actors were sought by the Federal Theatre. The Harlem Experimental Theatre presented and was supported by artists in other fields, among them Charlotte Wallace Murray, soloist at Riverside Church, pianist Elizabeth Sinkford, and Edna Guy, dancer and former pupil of Ruth St. Denis.

In conclusion I would like to add a final observation: One of the early pioneer theatres was the Howard University Players under the direction of Montgomery Gregory. This group really gave Negro theatre movements a boost, and I think this greatly influenced Dr. DuBois' efforts with Krigwa. He had hoped that more of these little theatres would be established across the country. Because of the record of Montgomery Gregory and the Howard Players, many former Howard students living in New York City rallied round and cooperated with Dr. DuBois in establishing a theatre similar to the Howard Players.

This type of pioneering is reflected in praiseworthy groups on the West Coast, the Free Southern Theatre, Detroit Theatre groups, Powell Lindsay's Suitcase Theatre in Michigan, the work of Baraka in New Jersey, Karamu House in Cleveland, and the work of men and women in Washington and other areas. Many little theatre groups dreamed of so very long ago are still extant, and the work goes on and on.

When some persons learned that I was taping material for this book, the question was immediately thrown at me: "Do you object to what's being done now"? Let me state that I am *not* against what drama groups are doing now. People live diverse lives. Therefore, there must be a diversity in what we produce. I think we must have a variety of life-styles and experiences revealed theatrically and in depth.

It gives me a great deal of personal satisfaction to have lived to see much of what we and other pioneers worked to achieve becoming a reality. However, we need more and more opportunities for our actors, writers and directors. Unlike Alexandre Dumas' hero, we as individuals cannot quite say, "The world is mine."

However, I believe we shall have the necessary opportunities before too many more years slip by.

Dick Campbell

A Voice: Dick Campbell

In previous essays I have described Dick Campbell and his late wife, Muriel Rahn, as my dramatic parents. They were well-known theatrical figures when I was playing stickball on the Harlem streets. And they lived directly across from us on 118th Street and Morning-side Avenue.

The first time I really got to talk to him was after a bunch of us had put on a terrible show at the Elks Auditorium on 129th Street. St. Clair Bourne, father of the filmmaker of the same name, reviewed our work for the *Amsterdam News* and he was very kind to us. If you didn't think we young cats were sharp, all you had to do was ask us.

Well, we heard about a black radio station being set up in the Alhambra Ballroom, so we went up there one night, ready to show the management that we were, indeed, God's gifts to the theatre.

We were so sharp you could have cut your fingers on the creases in every living cat's trousers. The chicks were so beautiful that a cat could taste lipstick by just looking at his chick.

We were sharp, sharp, sharp and we were going to save the theatre!

We made our grand entrance, but no one noticed us. The people in the ballroom were busy listening to W. C. Handy, composer of the *St. Louis Blues*, play his trumpet. Then, the people listened to Mr. Handy talk about the need for a black radio station. Dick Campbell was the master of ceremonies and he handled that microphone with professionalism. He had the audience in his hands and he broke up the place.

We young saviours of the theatre bowed our heads. We saw the professionals at work and we knew we were out of our league. We were caught between Joe

Louis' left jab and Muhammad Ali's right. The creases vanished from our now baggy trousers and the lipstick worn by the chicks seemed to smear.

We also got a course in true professionalism and humility. During the intermission Dick Campbell recognized my brother Clayton, and he came over and joined our group. He said:

"It certainly does my heart good to see a bunch of youngsters interested in the theatre. Congratulations!"

We were wasted. All we could do was humbly thank him. Then came the knock-out punch—as if one were needed. Mr. Campbell said:

"Can any one of you kids do a specialty? I'll put you on the program and you can publicize your group."

If you ever saw a bunch of militants do a soft-shoe shuffle, then you know what happened. We had a quick conference and decided that Juanita Coles, sister of Honi Coles, who was then a tap dancer, would sing a number. Poor Juanita found herself practically pushed to the stage. Mr. Campbell introduced her, introduced the group, and Juanita sang beautifully.

We learned that night that the true professional is a big, big man, always willing to help a newcomer. True, you have some real dogs, but you find them in all walks of life. Mr. Handy spent time with us, encouraged us to keep going, and Mr. Campbell spent more time with us. And so did all of the other professionals there.

For many years after that I had nightmares about what might have happened had we walked in there, stopped everything and said: "We are here to save you old folks!"

Not too long after that I learned another lesson from Dick Campbell. I was riding the bus across 116th Street and he was on the bus. He came up to me and said he was happy to see youngsters interested in the theatre. He invited me to join the Rose McClendon Players and learn whatever I could. I was delighted. I joined and he cast me in the black version of *Having Wonderful Time.*

I was scared out of my wits. This was the Depression and here I was, a kid dealing with professionals. But fear makes us sometimes put on airs and I did just that. I went around letting every one know that I was working with Dick Campbell and Muriel Rahn. I name-dropped them all over Harlem.

You saw it coming. The pitch was right down the middle of the plate and I took a called third strike. It came because I name-dropped in front of a chick I knew and I was trying to jive that fine chick. But I did not get to first base with her. In fact, I did not get to home plate. She tagged me "Out" before I could get to the bat-rack.

But this time I knew I was going to hit the long ball because she wanted to be an opera singer. She asked me to get her into Mr. Campbell's group. I said: "Oh, yes, Baby. I'll use my influence with Dick."

Well, I talked to Dick Campbell and I did *not* call him Dick. I asked him if he would hear this young lady read and he agreed to do so. I took that chick up to rehearsal at the New York Urban League and Mr. Campbell gave her a nice role. I was on my way around the bases, ready to score.

I told you that I was about to learn a lesson. I did. One time I called for the chick to go to rehearsal, she decided she wanted me to take her to the movies. Like a fool I did. The next time I went to take her to rehearsal she decided she wanted me to take her to another movie. I did.

I did not take her to another movie. The next day when I got home Mr. Campbell was sitting up in my living room, talking to my mother and my father. You see, I did not fully appreciate that the black community and the intellectual community are very small, indeed. I had even forgotten that Mr. Campbell knew my parents.

Icy stares greeted me as I walked into the room. Furthermore, our Harlem home has one of those long hallways that you walk up to from the front door. In other words, I did not have running room. I had been caught and I braced myself for the slaps in the face. They did not come, but I wish they had. I heard three lectures from three people—all about time in the theatre being money, about partying and getting up and taking care of business, about the meaning of work and the joy of doing anything well, which requires work, about all work being hard work and everything else. You name it and I heard it.

My mother and father had a few things to say about the theatre being serious business, about it being white-controlled and that a black man needed to know a lot to work in it. And you did not work at it half-way.

That was thirty-five years ago and I have never been late nor skipped another rehearsal since that day.

Dick Campbell. I could write a book about the man Ossie Davis and I call Big Daddy. But I couldn't tell it the way this tall, dynamic, brilliant man could tell it. I knew that he came out of Texas, went to Prairieview College, where he played football, and Paul Quinn College, then on into show business. He was a singer, a straight man, actor, social worker, writer, concert-artist manager, actor's agent, director, producer, public relations man, and today he is executive director of the

Sickle Cell Disease Foundation of Greater New York. He came to New York City in the 1920's, played in shows at various Harlem theatres and on Broadway in *Hot Chocolates*, *Singing the Blues*, *Brainsweat* and *Cabin in the Sky*. He also served as the American National Theatre Academy's representative to Africa, directed the office of public information for Operation Crossroads Africa for the late James Robinson. He was one of the first black men to cross the color bar of the general manager's union on Broadway and he handled such productions as Langston Hughes' *Tambourines to Glory* and my show *Ballad for Bimshire*.

But, most of all, I remember him as a beloved friend —a father-figure. Big Daddy! He taught me what the theatre was all about. I would read or see this or that play and run up to his house at any hour of the night and sit and discuss the meaning, the style, the form of the play. He picked me up when I was down. He borrowed five hundred dollars once and stuck it in my hands and it took me three years to repay him. And he never said a word about it.

He introduced me to people who promoted my career and produced my plays: Ossie Davis, Frederick O'Neal, Alain Locke, Duke Ellington, Fredi Washington, Billy Rowe, George Norford, Milton Quander, Freddie Carter, Langston Hughes, W. C. Handy, Guthrie McClintic, Willie Bryant, Ralph Cooper, Pigmeat Markham, Moms Mabley, Andy Razaf and scores of others.

Whatever I am now, he is responsible for it in dramatic terms. So—how do you say thank you and introduce a man like Dick Campbell?

I do not write that well.

THE WORDS OF
Dick Campbell

When I agreed to participate in this venture, I thought I would deal first with an incident that happened in Philadelphia in the early thirties. I was working with my late wife, Muriel Rahn, a beautiful soprano who was just getting started on a long singing career. She later became the original Carmen of Billy Rose's *Carmen Jones.*

We were a singing team at the time, and we had been hired to do the singing chores in a stage production by Ralph Cooper called *Chocolate Blondes.* The black girls wore blonde wigs in the show, so you see the blonde Afros worn by the ladies on 125th Street in Harlem today are not necessarily new.

There were two theatres in Philadelphia where black people played in those days. One was on Lombard Street called The Lincoln and the other was on South Street called The Standard. We were playing The Lincoln, which was run by a man called Slatko.

Mr. Slatko had a bad reputation among black performers. He very often failed to pay the performers the money he had agreed to pay them and a contract didn't mean a thing to him.

He had agreed to pay the Rahn-Campbell team $150 for the week. But when payday came, he came up short. He claimed the show didn't "draw" that week, but he would give us $75 anyway.

I was sort of expecting something like this, and was furious. I said: "Oh no! You'll pay me what my contract calls for, $150."

He said: "Well, you take this 75 bucks and don't bother me. Get the hell out!"

I said: "OK, Mr. Slatko, but I'll be back!"

I really didn't know what to do. But I had to do something. The man had robbed me. I wanted to

attack him, but that would only land me in jail. I
wanted to expose the man to the black audience, but
how? I went backstage and told my wife what happened. She too became furious. "The whole world
should know how this man treats black performers,"
she said. And that gave me an idea. Tell everyone
about him. But first, create a commotion of some sort.
I went outside and something told me to set the fire
alarm off. I did. But that wasn't enough. There was a
police telephone on the corner so I called the police
and reported there was a riot at this theatre. In about
15 minutes nearly 150 cops showed up in police wa-
gons. Fire department trucks gathered all around the
theatre. People crowded around and nobody knew
what was going on.

I pointed at Slatko when the fire chief asked:
"Where's the fire?"

"There's the fire," I said, "and he started it. He didn't
pay me my money!"

When the police chief wanted to know where the
riot was, I told him *I* was rioting because I had been
robbed!

Naturally, I got my money.

That incident is amusing in retrospect, but it under-
lines what I am certain is a continuing theme in this
volume. That theme is the rape of the black theatrical
heritage and the constant robbing and exploiting of
black artists.

But all of my Philadelphia experiences were not like
the one I just mentioned. I remember the Standard
Theatre. The back of the theatre was on Decatur
Street and the front was on South Street. And one
thing about the Standard Theatre was this: If the
people didn't like you, it was easy for you to make

your exit onto Decatur Street and keep going. This was true of a lot of other theatres, too.

I played the whole Toby circuit (Theatrical Bookers and Owners Association) in my time, mostly by accident. I was with one of the best Toby shows that existed in the late twenties and thirties: the Whitman Sisters' Show. The Whitman Sisters—Bert and Alice Whitman—came through once a year in all of the towns of the South. I remember I came from California and joined them in 1928. They were in Kansas City. I was playing a speakeasy in Kansas City in those days—one called the White Horse Tavern. This was one of those speakeasies where you sing from seven o'clock at night till seven in the morning. And I mean straight. One of the men who played the White Horse then was named Count Basie. Another was Coleman Hawkins from St. Joe, Missouri. All of us were around there about that time.

But I joined the Whitman Sisters' Show in Kansas City in 1928. It seems that Bert Whitman had had a little "amour" going with her straight man, Tony Grant. They broke up. The show needed a singer and a straight man. The chap who was the stage manager for the show was a young fellow named Willie Bryant. Willie asked me to work in place of Tony Grant. So, I joined the Whitman Sisters and we went on that season and played every town of any consequence in the South—Atlanta, Birmingham, Louisville, Houston, St. Louis, Kansas City. All of the towns in the South and in the Midwest. We came on into New York and Willie Bryant and I quit the show at the same time.

Then began the days of the Alhambra Theatre in New York where they had dramatic sketches interspersed in between the musical portions of the show.

The Alhambra was located at 126th Street and Seventh Avenue. The building is still there. I noticed in passing there recently that the windows are being torn out. I suppose they'll erect another building there.

Eddie Hunter, one of the contributors to this volume, played a comedy sketch there with Tim Moore. Tim later scored in the television version of *Amos and Andy*.

Now, a word about those comedians back there in those days. In 1926 I was in California and there were two comedians who were the forerunners of Amos and Andy. This was another white team called Moran and Mack, "The Two Black Crows." They had a record out that was a tremendous success.

A funny thing about black people in those days: They bought more of those records than they bought records that black people did. And Amos and Andy were, I suspect, as popular—or more popular—among black people than they were among other people. I guess this was because we as a people had been conditioned to the kind of inferior type of entertainment we had grown accustomed to seeing or the imitative type of comedy spoken of in Loften Mitchell's *Black Drama*. We felt we were relegated to this type of comedy that existed until very recently. So, comics Moran and Mack, the "Two Black Crows," were the forerunners of Amos and Andy, who became one of the most popular and I suppose one of the most wealthy teams that ever existed.

But, back in those days "Toby-time" was a great training ground for our performers. I remember even in my hometown in Beaumont, Texas, I saw a company led by Doc Strain. He was a tall, lanky, brown-skinned man who was more of a manager than a performer. He always had a good show. He toured the South and played in tents. Even in my hometown. Later when I was in Los Angeles in the early twenties, a new Lincoln Theatre opened on Central Avenue and about Thirty-second Street. Doc Strain's show opened the Lincoln Theatre. He had a stock company. He did the same type of show that he did on the road in the South, but it lasted a long time there. Some of the comedians that he had were Johnny Lee Long, Bootsie, and a number of others.

Mr. Campbell's comments about Amos and Andy and Moran and Mack certainly have validity. To this date one can hear such folk expressions as "that thing failed because it was an Amos and Andy venture," or an inept institution is often called a "Fresh Air Taxi Cab Company."

Many black Americans were also unaware of the stereotypes created by such comedians. Brilliant men and women have reported that, when they heard these comics, they laughed, not realizing the humor was directed at *them*. Godfrey Cambridge documents their point when he tells the story about getting on a bus in suburbia and a prejudiced white woman screams: "Negroes! Negroes!" Godfrey promptly jumps up in dismay and asks: "Where? Where?"

In 1957 the great *New York Times* critic, Brooks Atkinson, put it another way when he said: ". . .humor is an indigenous part of Negro plays. It helps to explain how the race has withstood its long travail without having a nervous breakdown. For Negroes can laugh, cynically no doubt, at the irony of their situation in America and . . . they can also laugh at their own foibles."

It is a bit difficult for me to talk about theatre without bringing up personal experiences and incidents that might be tied in with people whom I have come in contact with in the theatre and whom I feel made some contributions along the way. As far back as I can remember, I have had an interest in theatre and—before I knew it myself—I was in it in one form or another. In my early youth I knew people who had been in the theatre, tent shows and medicine shows, and all of this old Americana of years ago inspired me and interested me and made me want to be in theatre. When I finished college and went to California—which was in the days of Prohibition and speakeasies—I got thrown somehow into that kind of life and theatre. I started in nightclubs and a number of people that are popular today were there then. For instance, there was a drummer that worked in a nightclub with me in the Bronx Palm Gardens. Now, why would a nightclub in Los Angeles be called the Bronx Palm Gardens? I never knew anything such as the Bronx existed because I had not yet been to New York, but there was in this Bronx Palm Gardens a guy by the name of Lionel Hampton, playing in a band run by a chap named Les Hite, a saxophonist who was quite a musician in his day. Lionel had never heard of a vibraphone at that time and I can attest to that.

These nightclub shows were extremely popular with Hollywood people and actresses like Norma Talmadge would come to Sebastian's Cotton Club, as it was called, in Culver City, California, along with her husband and Rudolph Valentino, the great film star. And there was Pola Negri, another great star. And there was another woman who staged the shows at Sebastian's Cotton Club. Her name was Carolyn Snowden and I recall her as being a tall, beautiful woman with a tremendous amount of talent. She could produce shows that ran from six to ten weeks at the Cotton Club. She was succeeded later by a team called Bromfield and Greeley. All of these were black people who had a great deal to offer.

Then a young man named Louis Armstrong appeared there, singing "Exactly Like You" and "Sunny Side of the Street."

There was a band called Curtis Mosby's Blue Blowers and it played at Solomon's Dance Hall in Los Angeles with a pianist named Henry Starr. Henry Starr was the forerunner of the chap today who plays with Mabel Mercer—Bobby Short. He was that type of piano player and artist. There was a budding radio station in Los Angeles called KYW and, of course, we found it necessary to use earphones with radio. I remember I used to sit in Waco, Texas, when I was in Paul Quinn College, with earphones on listening to the Kansas City Nighthawks playing. And we had just gotten out of the earphone stage shortly after I got to California.

Henry Starr was one of the leading pianist-singers in those days. Few ever heard of him, perhaps, but he was a fine artist, a fine pianist, a fine singer. Curtis Mosby's Blue Blowers was one of the great recording bands of that era.

I left California after about two years there and I was exposed to a lot of people in nightclubs. Eddie Rucker, one of the first drug addicts I saw in my life, worked in nightclubs and seemed to alternate between Los Angeles and Tijuana. Those were the days of the real old speakeasy, or early nightclub, singers and Eddie used to do a bit which was very realistic: He would sing the song "I'm Always Chasing Rainbows," and he would do his drug-addict scene where he was shown sniffing coke. It always got a big hand. We always said: "Eddie was only doing what he did naturally."

I had heard about New York, but we migrated to Kansas City first, where I worked with Count Basie and Coleman Hawkins and then joined the Whitman Sisters' Show. I became the leading man. I had a tenor voice in those days and I worked with a soprano singer who had been a schoolteacher. This work carried me all over the country.

It was really an experience to be exposed to audiences that were the kind that related to what you did. While it was always predominantly a black audience, we never felt insecure about what we were doing. We always tried to do whatever we were doing in a very professional way. Out of this theatre—this "Toby-time" circuit—almost every black comedian, performer and artist got his training. This was bread and butter to a lot of people. It had to be that way because theatre was a segregated institution, just as every other institution was segregated. You developed your own in those days: black professional people, black schools, black everything and white everything. But, it was illuminating to me to come to New York City and become involved in the New York theatre.

Somehow, though, with all the experience I had had, with all the participation I had experienced over the years—well, they were never really satisfactory to me. Although I thought I sang well and I thought I performed well, I was never really satisfied with what happened and what went on in the theatre for blacks.

For a number of years before 1942 I appeared in

Broadway shows with high-caliber people like Ethel Waters, Bill Robinson and others. But I never really thought that black people achieved in the theatre what they were capable of achieving.

Another problem I had in the theatre was my complexion. I was considered a bit "too light" to qualify for some of the roles black people had to portray. I felt that as a black man I was not achieving what I could achieve and I made up my mind to do something about it. I knew that among black people there was as much going on as there was in any other ethnic group in the world. This was crying for presentation somewhere. Then, I met a woman named Rose McClendon in 1931 or 1932 and we decided to do something about it.

We organized what became known as the Negro People's Theatre. A few of us—Dorothy Paul, a chap by the name of Whitfield, Rose McClendon—produced a play by Clifford Odets called *Waiting for Lefty* at the Rockland Palace in 1935. About five thousand people jammed Rockland Palace and we were off and running.

Shortly afterwards Rose McClendon died. We sort of halted, but then we continued a couple of years later when I set up the Rose McClendon Players, which continued right on up to 1941. I founded this group because I felt, as I said before, that there was much to be written and much to be done by black people in the theatre. It had not been done. I made a statement at the time and it was carried by the black press. I said: "Black people might as well forget about Broadway. They had better stay off Broadway. They had better never, never, never again try to get anything on Broadway that will bring credit to black people. As a people we have to do something ourselves." Although that was back in 1937, the strange thing is that it is being said today. When I hear C.O.R.E. and Roy Ennis and all those people talking about black people, I say: "These boys are just about thirty years late."

I said this thirty years ago. I meant it in a different light, however. I didn't mean we had to segregate ourselves, or that we had to be isolating ourselves. What I meant was that we had to do things ourselves. We had to develop our talent, develop our own theatre, our playwrights and everything else. We had to interpret our way of life to the public because the public had never seen it. The public had only seen what Hollywood or Broadway had given out about black people.

Mr. Campbell's thirty-year-old statement is applicable today. Even with the upsurge of plays about black Americans and the lush black film market, one has to look very hard to find dramatizations of black historical figures. In fact, one needs a magnifying glass. It appears as though the mass media is willing to concede "pop" stuff to the black artist and ignore the in-depth work of black pioneers of this nation.

So, we tried to produce something, but unfortunately at first we looked around for material written by black playwrights and we could find none. We had to resort to some warmed-over Broadway plays. One of the first that we did was *Goodbye Again* by Allan Scott and George Haight. We didn't change anything. We just did it. Then we did *Having Wonderful Time*, which Loften Mitchell appeared in. We did that and finally we moved to the Mt. Morris Park Library on 124th Street and Fifth Avenue.

The librarian, Carolyn Thorne, said we could use the library basement which had been set up by some W.P.A. workers. The place had a dimmer board, curtains and a small pinhead stage. The auditorium seated seventy-five people, so we adopted that as our home. There we did Abram Hill's *Striver's Row* and George Norford's *Joy Exceeding Glory*, and an allegory about Booker T. Washington, which was taken to the 1939 World's Fair and done on the American Commons. It was also where we did another play called *Yellow* and one called *Black Woman in White*, and there was also Ferdinand Voteur's *A Right Angle Triangle*.

All these plays that are being done today about black people—well, people had better watch out when they say: "It's the first black play." Because it isn't.

The first black plays were done by black people, even before I did any. There was W. E. B. DuBois' group, the Krigwa Players, and Regina Andrews and the Harlem Experimental Theatre, and if you want to go back, you can go back to the founding of this country. But, I think the first time modern producers got excited about our work was when we did plays at the Rose McClendon Players' Workshop and the American Negro Theatre. They got excited to the point that when they saw *Anna Lucasta* done by the American Negro Theatre, they said: "There is something here that is salable." So, all the interest there is today in the black theatre and the black movie, all of that began thirty years ago. It did not just start. It has been quite an experience over the years.

Now, the handicap of the Rose McClendon Players —apart from money—was getting scripts. Then, there was the necessity of educating and organizing audiences and doing what the Theatre Guild had, beginning in 1919. That was getting subscription audiences. I think we may have had the first theatre in Harlem to organize subscription audiences. We charged two dollars for four plays and we built up an audience of about one hundred and fifty to two hundred people. My late wife, Muriel Rahn, worked very hard at that all the time. Between the two of us we kept things going and sometimes we had to dig into our pockets to do so. But, you see that out of that came people like Ossie Davis and Helen Martin. And when the late Dooley Wilson did Booker T. Washington for me, Ethel Waters came to see the show and she took him with her into *Cabin in the Sky.* From there Dooley went on to play with Humphrey Bogart and Ingrid Bergman in the movie *Casablanca.* In that he sang the song "As Time Goes By." Yes, there were contributions and recognition that came as a result of our kind of theatre.

We had some very fine writers come out of that group: Ossie Davis, J. Homer Tutt, Sidney Easton, Warren Coleman and many, many more. One of the fine playwrights was Abram Hill. I first produced his *Striver's Row* back in 1938. I recognized at that time that this was a type of writing by a black playwright that would eventually find a place in the American theatre.

It had not yet found a place in the American theatre because all the work we had seen about black people in the theatre and in the movies had been more or less stereotyped characters—whether in comedy, drama or anything else. There were certain strictures that the entertainment media had to adhere to.

I thought Abram Hill with his *Striver's Row* broke through for the first time, and it is sad that he happened to be about thirty years before his time.

Another playwright we had and that we haven't heard from since was George Norford. He wrote a play called *Joy Exceeding Glory*—a take-off on one of our cultists, if you may call Father Divine that. We've had plenty before and since. I thought George was an excellent playwright with a future, but he never continued because I feel that he, too—like many black playwrights—knew that opportunities were extremely limited. They weren't putting anything on Broadway in those days that would make black playwrights rich. If you wrote anything, it had to be something that was in the mold, that white audiences would buy.

Another artist with us in those days was Frederick O'Neal. He played in five or six of our shows. Later Abram Hill and Fred O'Neal started the American Negro Theatre, which made a great contribution to Broadway. It was just coming of age with *Anna Lucasta*, which had unforgettable performances by Hilda Simms and Fred.

During World War II, I left the Rose McClendon Players and in 1942 took over the United Services Organization Camp Shows. They looked around for people to do this kind of show, the kind I had been in in vaudeville. There was a shortage of producers just as there was a shortage of playwrights. They gave me the job because Noble Sissle—who was in the USO Camp Show set-up—was not interested in producing. He was interested in another production of his fine show, *Shuffle Along*. Now, one of the amusing things about all of that was when artist Earl Sweeting walked

into my office one day with a check amounting to
something like $45,000. That was my payroll. Sweeting
had found the check that the bank messenger or
somebody had lost someplace. He got no money for
his honesty, but we had a press conference and
praised Earl for what he had done. Someone once
said Sweeting's history is replete with making head-
lines and big news, but little money.

To get back to theatre, movies, and black people is
to get to Oscar Micheaux, a pioneer black film-maker.
Just shortly after Oscar started his work, Hollywood
got on the black bandwagon and made a couple of
black movies. One was *Hallelujah* with Nina Mae
McKinney, Bill Fountaine and Daniel Haynes. Then
there was another movie called *Hearts in Dixie* with
Stepin Fetchit. These two movies were similar in type
and I think one company did it to compete with the
other company. *Hallelujah* opened at two theatres in
New York: one downtown and the other uptown.

Why did they have two openings? The reason was
they didn't want too many black people coming
downtown to see this movie. That was in 1929.

Simultaneously, on Broadway was *Connie's Hot
Chocolates*, which had premiered at Connie's Inn on
131st Street and Seventh Avenue in Harlem. I was
in that show, singing opposite Margaret Sims, and the
song we introduced in the show later became popular.
This was "Ain't Misbehavin'," popularized by Louis
Armstrong.

A funny thing happened in that show. Louis Armstrong and Fats Waller were in the show and they
opened the second half. There were Louis, Fats, and
singer Edith Wilson. Louis had just come into the
show because we felt that after we opened at the

Windsor Theatre in the Bronx, the show needed a lift. The producers sent to Chicago and brought Louis here. The young trumpet player was making it, all right. He had cut some good records for Okeh Records and everyone knew he was on his way to greatness.

Louis and Fats opened the second half of the show with the theme song, "Ain't Misbehavin'." Fats clowned on stage and when they got to what we call the channel or the middle part of the song, Louis forgot the lyrics. He was singing: "Ain't misbehavin', I'm savin' all my love for you . . ." and then he got to the middle part and he sang: "Dum de dum and I done forgot the words, and I don't know what to do. . ." and this business of "I done forgot the words and . . ." went over big with the audience that night. This was what became known as scat singing. The producers came backstage and said: "Keep that in! Forget the words every night!" And later when Louis cut the record, he had to "forget the words" just as he had forgotten them on stage. So—what was an accident became a permanent thing. That was one of the highlights of *Hot Chocolates*.

Now, Andy Razaf who wrote the lyrics didn't mind this at all. Andy and Harry Brooks were the lyricist and composer for *Hot Chocolates*, although Fats Waller was in on it, too. That was a good show. Comedian Eddie Green was in it and I later worked with him. That was the following year: Eddie was the comedian and I was his straight man. I think we became the first black comedy team to play radio. We played the Fleischmann Yeast Hour with Rudy Vallee in 1930 and 1931. We did about five consecutive weeks with him. We were mentioned prominently

as highlights like they do now for television shows—
"Green and Campbell."

We worked a lot of radio after that. Eddie Green
never got the recognition for his greatness that I
thought he deserved. Eddie Hunter will tell you that
Green wrote well. He wrote a lot of material. He was
a graduate of the burlesque theatre and he came on
strong.

There were other plays that I had the opportunity
of being in and observing. There was a musical called
Singing the Blues. I don't know whether many people
remember that, but it appeared in 1931. Starring in
that play were Frank Wilson, Isabell Washington,
and her sister, Fredi Washington. One of the fellows
who came backstage nightly to see Isabell was a
young man named Adam Clayton Powell, Jr. He later
married Isabell and, of course, he later became the
famous Harlem congressman. Then there were other
shows like *Hot Rhythm* with Bill Robinson. That
played the Times Square Theatre on Broadway in
1930. Lots of other plays came and went quickly, very
quickly. There was Garland Anderson's *Appearances.*
I saw the very first performance of that in Los Angeles
in 1927. It came onto Broadway a few years later.
Then, there was a play by Wallace Thurman called
Harlem, and I suppose this was the first Harlem play
that was done. We've seen a lot of so-called Harlem
plays since, but I think this might have been the first
of the crop.

In 1935 I had a traumatic experience. I never really
got over it, but it told me I had to get out of the
performing end of the theatre. Casting was on for
Porgy and Bess and a casting agent named Margaret

Linley had seen my work. She was with the Theatre Guild then and she had seen me do an imitation of Cab Calloway in those days. Cab was the choice of the Theatre Guild to do the character Sportin' Life in *Porgy and Bess*. But, Cab was not available. He had a big band in those days and was making big money. And he asked for big money for *Porgy and Bess*.

Nobody was certain *Porgy and Bess* was going to be a success and it was *not* during its initial run. It ran, I think, about twelve weeks. But, anyway, I was the poor man's Cab Calloway at that time, so I auditioned and made it for all the producers and directors until George Gershwin came on the scene. Gershwin turned me down. He said:

"What the boy does is all right, but he's not what I want."

And I wasn't. He got Bubbles. John Bubbles. Gershwin wanted a tap dancer like Bubbles to do Sportin' Life and not the Cab Calloway type. I lost out.

I decided along about that time that Broadway was not for me. Shortly after that, I set about organizing the Rose McClendon Players and went on from there.

By 1942 we had finished. I went into *Cabin in the Sky* with Ethel Waters. The last thing we put on at the Rose McClendon workshop was a show called *Gospel Train*, written by J. Homer Tutt. Years before I had seen J. Homer Tutt in my hometown, Beaumont, Texas, in a show called *A Smart Set* and the year was 1916 or 1917. I was a kid and this show was at the Kyle Theatre. I saw these black performers singing and dancing and I said: "Boy, that's what I've got to do. One of these days. . ." and every day I would go

down to the train station and watch the Southern
Pacific roll through town. I'd say: "One of these days
I'm going to be on that Southern Pacific going to
California or somewhere." And I did.

Now, one thing that ought to be stated here was
the constant attempt on our part to bring the vitality,
the rhythms, the life-styles of the black community
into focus. This is what was recognized a long time
ago and with my directorial efforts I always had that
in mind. This vitality, this drive, this rhythm and life-
style could be found in the work of the straight men
who came out of "Toby-time"—Jimmy Baskette, Mon-
te Hawley, Johnny Vigal, Billie Andrews, Willie Bryant. And all of this was evident in the artistry of
Bessie Smith, Mamie Smith, Ma Rainey, Dusty Fletch-
er, Gallie DeGaston.

I must mention Moms Mabley. I first remember her
as Jackie Mabley at the Lafayette Theatre. This talented comedienne was always in the presentations, not
the dramas. And today Moms Mabley is possibly the
highest paid of black television performers.

And another thing. We were not being *funded* in
those days. That word did not exist back then. I recall
a very unusual incident, a pathetic one, really. I
wanted to produce George Norford's play, *Joy Exceeding Glory*, which had been written while George was
a student at Columbia, in the Brander Matthews Theatre. He was the only black student in the playwriting
class. Well, Hatcher Hughes and Milton Smith, directors of the Brander Matthews Theatre, did not want to
"black-up" the white students to do George Norford's
play. They came over to Harlem and asked me to do
George's play. That's how I got hold of *Joy Exceeding
Glory*.

I told Milton Smith that what he should do was try to get me a grant. He was agreeable and said he would try. I could then go on and get a master's degree in directing and playwriting. He tried. He applied to the General Education Fund, and they said: "No. We are not in the business of theatre or in the business of training people for the theatre." They turned me down. But, the point is that since then that's all the business they've been in—underwriting people in the theatre with grants and so forth. I have often thought that had just a little bit of help been offered, black theatre artists might have developed a great deal faster and better than we did. We just appeared at the wrong time.

The Federal Theatre did help the black artist in many ways, but again—this was the Open-the-Door-to-Black-People-and-Shut-It-Fast policy. I was the last director of the Federal Theatre and I lasted exactly four weeks. Because in four weeks Congress killed that theatre. Hallie Flanagan appointed me director of the Federal Theatre in Harlem in June, 1939, and by the end of June an Act of Congress destroyed the Federal Theatre.

I know someone is going to ask me what I consider my shining hour. To that I can only say that what impresses me more than anything else are the people who came out of our theatre, the people I once performed with in one way or another and who have gone on to great things. Ossie Davis spent five years with me. And people like Eddie Hunter and Frederick O'Neal and Abram Hill and the editor of this volume, who mentioned some contributions I might have made in his writing. This means something to me.

In fact, it makes all the hardships worthwhile.

Abram Hill

A Voice: Abram Hill

Abram Hill and Frederick O'Neal organized the American Negro Theatre while I was away at college.

Abe had written *Striver's Row*, a wonderful comedy, when I was with the Rose McClendon Players.* When I came home for summer vacation I heard that he had started rehearsing a new production of the play at the 135th Street Library.

Since I was going to be back in college by the time the show opened, Abe invited me to a rehearsal. And I am sure he was later sorry because in those days I had a big, hearty laugh and when I laughed, I laughed. Well, I laughed all over the theatre and Abe was too gentle to throw me out.

At the heart of Abe's play is the Van Striven family. They are black and they are very middle-class. Striver's Row is, of course, that beautiful group of houses on 137th Street, 138th Street and 139th Street, built by architect Stanford White. Writers—that is, well-paid writers—doctors, lawyers, dentists and other black and a number of white professionals live there as of this writing. But you have to strive to live on Striver's Row.

And the Van Strivens are striving. Dolly, the wife of Mr. Van Striven, is the declared leader of her social set. She gives her daughter a big coming-out party. Well, Mrs. Envy is Dolly's rival in this social set and she wants to break up the party and embarrass Dolly. So

* Note: At the time of its premiere, Abram Hill's well-known comedy was called *On Striver's Row*; some years later the author shortened the name to *Striver's Row*, and under this title it is still widely performed.

Mrs. Envy invites Joe Smothers, a jive-talking, hip character, to break up the party. The joint begins to jump as Joe carries on. He puts down some long Harlem talk. He has brought along a broad named Ruby and they begin to Lindy Hop and tear up the house.

Dolly is about to faint, but her maid from the country saves the day. She recognizes Joe Smothers and well she should, because she asks: "Honey, are those the new clothes I bought for you?" All Joe can say is "Damn Sam!" Furthermore, Joe is in hot water because he has Ruby there. He must confess to the maid that he is doing all of this for her because Mrs. Envy has paid him to break up Dolly's party. Joe and Ruby get out of there in a hurry because Dolly has her shoe off. As the second act curtain falls, Dolly has raised her shoe to Mrs. Envy's head, declaring:

"I am going to put some misery where it belongs!"

This is really an injustice to Abe Hill's play. You laugh, but you have tears in your eyes because he also deals with the black country maid who came north to be treated well by whites and blacks. And she is painfully hurt.

Few are the people who know enough to appreciate Abe Hill's marvelous play. Many a good, honest white critic has stubbed his toe trying to analyze the play. Ditto many black critics. I have only seen it six times so I am, of course, prejudiced in my point of view.

At the rehearsal I attended I was also delighted to see a young Harlem girl I knew in the cast. Her name was Ruby Wallace. Today she is known as Ruby Dee.

Well, after I had ruined the rehearsal, Abe was good enough to invite me to Henry's Sugar Bowl. We sat down and had malteds and then coffee and more coffee and we talked far into the night. He outlined the forthcoming production of *Native Son* on Broadway, broke down the meaning of scenes and offered insights into this work that I could hardly put into words.

This tall, gentlemanly scholar was prematurely bald. He had too much intelligence for hair to stay on his head. I truly admired and still admire Abe. He sacrificed having a family and poured everything he had into the building of an American Negro theatre in the Harlem area. And he had his heart broken.

For many people—big people and little people—went after Abe's head. Beloved friends began to ask him why he was famous and not rich. The pressure mounted, increasingly. No one bothered to look at his record: All he did was to found a theatre, sacrifice his writing career and his potential family for that cause, promote present-day stars like Sidney Poitier and Hilda Simms and Harry Belafonte, and such writers as Alice Childress. Many brought stories to me and I told them to go to hell. I was not going to get in the middle of downright jealousy. I despise small-minded people of all nations, races and creeds.

After rewriting and producing the black version of *Anna Lucasta,* he wrote the Harlem version and later the Broadway version of *Walk Hard.* He adapted a play known as *Miss Mabel,* wrote and produced a version of *The Power of Darkness,* and sponsored such plays as Theodore Browne's *Natural Man.* Finally, he could bear no more of insults and taunts and he left the American Negro Theatre to become a professor at Lincoln University in Pennsylvania. There he imported professional actors to work with college students. Eventually, he came home to New York City and he lives now in Harlem. The scars of all this and other rebuffs are on Abe's body. The hope here is that it is not too late for them to be healed. His very life is a record of attempting to do things for theatre artists.

It would be one of the ironies of theatrical history if this pioneer went along unnoticed. We need him and it is up to all of us to bring him back into the theatre to which he has contributed so very much.

THE WORDS OF
Abram Hill

I have not really been active in the theatre in almost twenty years. I call myself divorced from the theatre, but about two or three times a year my good friend, Loften Mitchell, tries to draft me back into the business. I took a cue from him some years ago when I invited him out to speak to a group, Workshop 59, I was directing in Springfield Gardens, Long Island, and he said—among other things—to the students: "Theatre is a jealous mistress. She will totally absorb you."

I began to realize how much I had been really involved in being absorbed in theatre, and I finally concluded that she is a jealous "bee"—and I don't have to tell you what that means.

In June, 1940, a group of us got together and organized the American Negro Theatre. There were many unusual things about that theatre, but I believe the unique thing was that we were probably the only theatre group in history that had to rehearse in a funeral parlor, because there wasn't any free space anywhere else in the community.

We had practically no money. I think at our first meeting we had eighteen people. We passed the hat around to collect money so we could send out cards to others who might be interested in our work. We collected a total of eleven cents. And that is how our theatre was started—with a great deal of enthusiasm, with the hope that we were going to solve all the problems that we were faced with in our theatre. Our people had many problems about the lack of participation in the commercial theatre. Many had a taste of the theatre in the W.P.A. setting. This federal program ended in 1939, leaving many looking for someplace to go. We were trying to work out and solve the problems of ourselves and find out if we could build a theatre of our own, although we had no money.

A.N.T. was an incorporated co-op, all members sharing the expenses and the profits. Expenses lived with us and the profits never visited us. In our eleven-year history, no one was paid any salary except for a period of three years when, under a grant of $22,000 from the General Education Board, part-time salaries were paid to the manager, the director and the secretary.

Despite the lack of financial assistance, this do-it-yourself enterprise managed to present fifteen major and five studio productions—and by major, I mean new scripts. Studio productions were of established scripts. We trained over two hundred people, attracted some fifty thousand patrons to witness 325 performances, and we raised enough money to finance these productions—with the largest gift coming from Mrs. Bill "Bojangles" Robinson, a gift of five dollars!

Financing a production for the hole-in-the-wall we called a stage was nevertheless a superhuman feat. So tiny was the stage that it was not on speaking terms with the pulpit of a storefront church. This pint-sized space fared well with our pint-sized budget. We spent $750 to $1,500 per production. Scenery, props, furnishings and other things for our small area were far less than those filling a larger, more orthodox stage. Fund raising from advance sales, subscription house parties, program ads, annual New Year's Eve parties, cut-rate theatre parties, guest appearances, and fines levied on delinquent members of the organization were some of the budget gimmicks we used. The enthusiasm, dedication and devotion of the members of A.N.T. rank exceptionally high on the theatre's ledger. Members executed all the tasks assigned to them, pleasant and unpleasant—including the driving through Harlem of a five-dollar-per-day rented horse and wagon that displayed ludicrous exaggerations of A.N.T. events. A medal for sharing might be awarded to a domestic by day and actress by night who brought leavings from a Bronx table to share with other undernourished members of our gang.

Misguided enthusiasm may foul up the best intentions. An overly solicitous salesman-actor, assigned to selling program ads, was guilty of printing an ad that was downright embarrassing. This unsavory bit of naivete escaped my circumspect eye. On an opening night I glimpsed critics Brooks Atkinson and Richard Watts, Jr., chuckling surreptitiously behind their programs over the following ad, which read:

"Hotel Blank, Rooms for Rent, by the day, by the week, or by the hour."

After the opening, the entire A.N.T. company remained until the wee hours, blocking out the word "hour" and inserting "month" in 5000 programs.

Despite the pitfalls that threatened and sometimes destroyed group practice at every turn, the A.N.T. heaved, wiggled and shook itself into a respectable experimental theatre. Attribute this to preparation. A.N.T. was not a group of black dilletantes dabbling on the periphery of sound theatre craft. Years of research, surveys, and the solutions to the problems inherent in this kind of activity predated the founding of the group. Ensemble playing, attuned almost in a musical manner; perfectionism in lieu of professionalism; thinking, artistic acting instead of the primitive natural; the development of supporting and responsive audiences were the ingredients that sparked critic John Chapman to tag A.N.T. as having: "The finest ensemble acting in town."

And I'm glad this book is to be published, for even now I get twenty to twenty-five letters a year—inquiries from people who are doing research or working on advanced degrees, people who want to know more about the birth, life and death of the A.N.T. It was born, lived and died in pursuit of some specific, dynamic aims.

Among the foremost aims was to destroy the black stereotypes. As one of its early members, Ruby Dee was the personification of this aim. She was unique, but so was her opponent—the eyeball-rolling, ghost-frightened pickaninny. I say unique, because in modern times it has been taken for granted that the actor on the stage was the equal of the member of the audience.

May I digress for a moment? May I read from a piece I wrote a while back? "All our arts—and particularly the theatre—have been infected by attitudes that were firmly established by chattel slavery. The theatre took over and encouraged the idea of an inferior group of people. Under the institution of slavery, one of the onerous tasks of the enslaved people was that of entertaining their masters. Southern planters were proud of their black slaves who could dance and sing, pick the guitar, clap bones, and sometimes play the violin. It is understandable that the minstrel show became an established entertainment in the American theatre, perpetuating in dramatic form the cruel notion of race inferiority. For the minstrel show was a unique form of theatre, in which the actors were inferior to the members of the audience. The minstrel show waned, unlamented, but the stereotype persisted in the forties, and substantial vestiges are still with us today—witness some black stylized and unreal characterizations—bad English, propensity for big words, and glut that erodes some revival scenes.

"Contravening the stereotype is the portrayal of individual character, with all the color, variety, dignity, pettiness, virtue and evil, and incredibly complex and contradictory motives that the individual is possessed of—whatever his complexion. Many black players bathe comfortably in any roles that they are fortunate enough to get. However, any honest and moderately serious actor-artist can tell you that this problem—the problem of assessing and portraying human character in relation to *his heritage and environment*—is the problem that obsesses his waking hours and haunts his dreams."

Sidney Poitier's movie characterizations have helped to bury the stereotype. His dignity, his sincerity, his imagination, and his sensitivity have made it possible for him as an actor to rise above the usual ineptly written characters he has portrayed.

His talent was vividly demonstrated at his *first* stage audition. As director of the A.N.T. and a member of its auditioning board—which included company manager Frederick O'Neal, apprentice director Osceola Archer, speech-voice specialist Doris Sorrell, and actress Alice Childress—I distinctly remember Mr.

Poitier's audition. Contrary to Hollywood legend, A.N.T. did not reject his first audition.

Without any dramatic flare, Sidney read an excerpt from *True Romance* magazine. Then I suggested that he forget the magazine and do an improvisation, giving him the following situation:

"You are a stranger in New York City. You are attending a dance at the Savoy Ballroom. You know none of the girls present. Approach one of them and ask for a dance. She refuses, but do all you can to convince her that she *must* dance with you. And she does."

After working out a routine in his mind, the 17-year-old acting candidate impressively approached an imaginary girl, who refused to swing with him. He made an instant transition, becoming the dashing man-about-town and exuding a natural charisma—which his victim could not resist. His metamorphosis was astonishing. Communicating in pantomime a few choice morsels of sweet talk, he and the girl danced away.

"Talented, uninhibited, expressive, coordinated. Accepted for membership. Needs training." This was what I wrote on his audition application. The screening board unanimously agreed to accept him in the apprentice group. It's been said this black superstar was at first rejected by the A.N.T. because of his West Indian speech. But his tryout was in pantomime and he passed without *talking* at all.

Ruby, Sidney, Hilda Simms and Harry Belafonte, along with other members, were intensely trained in acting, speech, voice, body movement and the fundamentals of theatre craft. This activity, combined with play production, took place in the cramped quarters of a Harlem library—where schedules sometimes extended beyond the 11 P.M. curfew and other spots had to be found to continue.

Frederick O'Neal, co-founder of A.N.T., often said at weekly meetings: "A.N.T. is not a star-making organization. One may play a leading role in one production and be an attendant in the rest room during the following presentation." Incidentally, there was only one rest room. The attendant doubled as a guard, seeing that only one gender at a time was accommodated.

Fred further said: "Stardom is a by-product of the highest individual achievement and can be bestowed upon you by ranks beyond this organization. *We* are a theatrical family. This family, not the individual, is the star."

Players inconveniently or conveniently met each acting class. In each miss-out, the delinquent had to dish out a two-bits fine.

The essence of A.N.T. training and its determination to portray black men and black women as MEN and WOMEN are shown in performances of the famous foursome.

Out of the pack of forty performers who had three years or more experience in A.N.T. approximately a dozen have acquired the featured players' tag, earn their bread—sometimes with butter—exclusively in "the trade." In this flock are: Frederick O'Neal, Helen Martin, Maxwell Glanville, Stanley Greene, Clarice Taylor, Gertrude Jeannette, Hilda Haynes, Pauline Myers, William Greaves, Alvin Childress, Jacqueline Andre and Isabelle Sanford.

Earle Hyman, an actor-artist of the same vintage as

the foursome, spent his first stage season with A.N.T. From the bit role of the Diaper Man in A.N.T.'s 1943 production of *Three's A Family*, Mr. Hyman, having mastered the Norwegian language, has earned such a hunk of acting honors that his replica now stands in the Norwegian Actors Hall of Fame.

Alice Childress, a so-called corn-on-the-cob colored actress who turned playwright because she lacked high visibility, is one of the A.N.T. alumnae who serve the theatre in a non-acting capacity. Other craftsmen are: Roy Allen, a television network technician; playwright-designer-director Roger Furman, who heads The New Heritage Theatre; black-theatre-research specialist Charles Griffin; Franklyn Thomas, director of the Harlem YMCA Players; playwright Oliver Pitcher; and Lou Smith, associated with the wardrobe department at the Yale University School of Drama. Novelist Ann Petry spent two years working with the A.N.T.

We had in mind another goal. Really we knew that we were blocked and the opportunities were limited. At that time we realized, too, that many stars who had made their debuts in *Mamba's Daughters* or *The Green Pastures* had not returned to Broadway in ten years or so. We said: "How can we look forward to participating in a situation in which there is little opportunity?" We said: "Let's do our own thing." So we pulled ourselves together and started building.

We eventually built up a subscription list of about fifteen hundred people who paid three dollars a year for three productions. I think Dick Campbell and the Rose McClendon Players had charged two dollars for four productions.

We had this little basement theatre in the 135th Street Library where we were welcomed for the first two or three years, and then eventually we were dispossessed. After presenting *Anna Lucasta*, which I will discuss later, we got reams and reams of publicity. Some of the publicity we got was considered negative by the library authorities. Critics would say: "In this small library basement, which is no larger than a big room, on this tiny vestpocket stage, these people have done thus and thus. . ." The library saw this as a kind of negative criticism of its facility. They said, in effect:

"We've helped you along so far. Now you can get out on your own."

We said: "But we haven't been paying any rent, haven't been paying any light bill, and we'd like to stay here."

We were given six months to get out. We finally found another location after about a year. We moved to the Elks Building, the Henry Lincoln Johnson Lodge, at 15 West 126th Street. And we did have the problem of paying $173 per month for rent. And the next thing that hurt us so badly was the fact that we had a light bill running from $175 to $200 a month. And the members began to ask: "Where's our money going?"

Incidentally, the Broadway run of *Anna Lucasta* beginning in 1944 did pay us 1¼ percent of the production, and out of that we saved up somewhere close to twenty thousand dollars within three years. But, after we moved into this new location and had these terrible rent and light expenses, the money dwindled and dwindled to about five thousand dollars in our treasury. It was, of course, difficult to sustain ourselves. We had to be sure that we had productions that would pay off because we depended almost exclusively on getting money from them to mount the next production.

The way we operated as a co-op was as follows: We paid 50 percent of the profit funds to the treasury of the organization and 50 percent would go to the members of the organization. I don't think we ever divided more than two hundred dollars among the entire company. Enthusiasm, we found, is no substitute for budget.

About 1943, Dr. Lawrence Reddick, then curator of the Schomburg collection which was housed in our same library building—came to me and said:

"The Rockefeller Foundation would like to talk to you."

I said: "For what?"

He said: "For money, of course."

I said: "Try to block my way!"

So I went down and talked to Jackson Davis of the General Education Board. He asked what we were doing and I went on and explained our program to him. He then wanted to know what we needed and my answer was:

"Money!"

He asked what we would do with the money if we had it. I told him we would put it into production, and that we would put two or three people on salary because we were all volunteering our services, doing this in the evening and supporting productions out of our own pockets. Some of our members had gone out and hocked their clothing or their jewelry. Actress Betty Haynes once pawned her grandmother's beautiful silver set. George Lewis pawned his grandmother's ring. I told Davis about these things.

Eventually we received the much-needed grant of $22,000.

We were concerned with new plays and we looked everywhere we could to find them. I wrote *Walk Hard* and *Striver's Row*, two out of the eleven original scripts we produced, and we produced plays written by black playwrights. We did Owen Dodson's *The Garden of Time* and Theodore Browne's *Natural Man*.

Also, we had a kind of floating directorship, although I was the executive director of the organization. What we were trying to do was—and I must say this idea came from Frederick O'Neal—create an organization in which all of us were so dedicated that no individual in the organization was stronger than the general membership, where everything was voted upon by a majority board, an executive board. The director had to abide by these rules and regulations. Mr. O'Neal has said that, in looking back, this was a bad idea. I know that now, too, but we were learning.

Membership in the A.N.T. included some actors with very light complexions. These "too white" blacks found double locks on Broadway doors. Broadway preferred highly visible black actors. Creating outlets for "pink" A.N.T.'s was another burden we assumed.

We were battling all kinds of wars. We were trying to eradicate from the scene the type of plays, the stereotyped plays that tended to demean the black people. Many times producers didn't realize what they were doing. They didn't seem to care too much because you didn't have that much black support on Broadway for anyone to be too concerned about it. Sometimes they'd call me up and say: "Abe, send me an actor." I'd say: "What type of actor do you want?"

The answer would include, among other requirements: "We want a well-done actor."

A well-done actor. That was the term which meant the producer wanted an ebony-colored actor. In other words, he did not want a light-complexioned actor. So they used the term "well-done."

Howard Lindsay and Russell Crouse visited me one day in 1944, looking for an actor. They had been scouting near the Tree of Hope and people had told them to go to the American Negro Theatre. They came to the theatre and walked in, saying "I'm Lindsay" and "I'm Crouse." They went on to tell me they were casting a play named *The Hasty Heart*. They said: "We want a big, burly Negro. You know the type."

I said: "Yes, but I don't have any. I do have a big actor but he's about the color of parched peanuts. Would you want him?"

They said: "Tell him to come to see us."

Robert Earl Jones, then known as Earl Jones, was doing a small part in our play *Walk Hard*. Earl had played the lead in Langston Hughes' *Don't You Want to Be Free?* at the Harlem Suitcase Theatre until he joined a Katharine Cornell Broadway-bound production. Then Albert Grant succeeded him. I told Earl to go down and see Lindsay and Crouse. He got the part.

When I learned he had the part, I asked: "How many lines do you have, Earl?" He said: "One word." He enjoyed a long run in the play that launched Richard Basehart toward stardom. The one word Earl spoke was "Blossom," the name of a Basuto native.

The Tree of Hope lingers in the folklore of Harlem. This was a huge tree that stood near 131st Street and Seventh Avenue, not too far from the site of the

Lafayette Theatre. The tree got its name because, according to folklore, a black actor stood under it once, hoping for work. Along came a theatre manager and he saw the actor. The manager promptly claimed that he had been looking for the actor and signed him to a contract. Thereafter, in the classic words of a number of Harlemites, "Every Negro actor and his brother who looked for work stood under the Tree of Hope."

In the 1930's when city authorities widened the avenue, the tree was cut down. Part of it was used at the 125th Street Apollo Theatre for the weekly radio show, *Amateur Night in Harlem*. It was mandatory for a competing amateur to walk on stage, touch the Tree of Hope, then begin performing. If an amateur did not touch that Tree, he was reminded to do so by the master of ceremonies and this was done in a loud, commanding manner. In short, touching the Tree was a religious rite.

The late, great tap dancer, Bill "Bojangles" Robinson, had the stump of the Tree of Hope placed on 131st Street and Seventh Avenue, directly in the mid-section of the avenue. There it stands as of this writing. The inscription reads: "To the people of Harlem. You wanted a Tree of Hope, so here 'tis. Bill Robinson."

That particular section remained for many years a gathering place for Negro performers. It is little wonder, then, that Howard Lindsay and Russell Crouse would visit that particular spot, seeking a Negro actor.

This story also makes a point about the changing nature of language with respect to race. For example, at one time the correct term to be used in terms of the black American was "coloured," then it became "Coloured," then "negro," and then, after Dr. DuBois' campaigns, the "N" was capitalized. In the 1930's the *New York Times* actually carried an editorial noting why it was capitalizing the "N" in Negro in the future. Now, of course, the term is "black" and polemics enter again, this time to support capitalizing the "B" in the word. This could go on and on, but one thing is emphasized here and that is that nomenclature and rhetoric do not change a *condition*.

As I've said, another feature we had in our organization was a revolving directorship. I tried to direct one show a year and then we would invite a guest director to do the other two. And, believe me, putting on one hit show a year was something I learned was a demanding assignment. The average Broadway producer gets one out of six, but here we were trying to do three a year, and we really had a tough time. We would hunt plays everywhere we could. We would write people and when we would finally get a script, every member would have to vote on it before we could do it. Most of our members were actors and unless they saw a part for themselves, they weren't interested in a script. So we managed to dig up plays and eventually a director. And finally we did one play in 1944 that made national and international history. That was *Anna Lucasta*.

Now, if anyone wants to know one of the high spots in my life, it was when *Anna Lucasta* clicked in that 135th Street Library basement theatre. During the intermission on opening night, I stepped out into the alley which faced our theatre entrance. There were two Broadway producers, battling over which of them would buy *Anna Lucasta* and take it to Broadway. Mind you, they were struggling over a product that I had "discovered." The punch line here is that they previously had treated me as if I were an office boy when I called on them.

Now, they fought. I laughed!

Anna was a history-making event. It put the organization on the map and ironically it planted the seeds of destruction. For, from that point on the organization was going downhill. People came into it after that, trying to get to Broadway. The A.N.T. became a showcase instead of an experimental theatre. All eyes focused on the bright lights of Broadway. Frederick O'Neal, Hilda Simms, Alice Childress, Alvin Childress, Earle Hyman, Georgia Burke and others were making it on Broadway via *Anna,* so everybody—that is, everybody but a few hard-core A.N.T.'s—went in that direction. There were people in the Harlem production who didn't go downtown. Some were quite sore. I think downtown took eight out of fourteen who had played uptown. And those that were left were never happy again.

Anna Lucasta was our smash hit. From two films and many English-speaking productions—and I think even a Yiddish version was done in Israel later—I can't imagine what this venture has really earned. I would have to say about twenty-five million. Within two years the play had grossed seven million through the national company and the local company. That much I know for a fact, for producer Jack Wildberg, according to a written agreement with A.N.T., sent us weekly statements.

We were getting 1¼ percent on only the Broadway production. People have said that we let Broadway take the play from us. That isn't exactly true. Philip Yordan, the author, gave us *carte blanche* in a contract arranged by play agent Claire Leonard because he and I mutually respected each other's talent. We were both playwrights under contract to Claire. About a year before we produced *Anna Lucasta*, she asked me to read a play named *Anna Lucaska*. The work was about a Polish-American family and Claire thought it would be a splendid vehicle for black actors. I read the script and told her: "I don't know. It's too much like O'Neill's *Anna Christie*." I asked Frederick O'Neal to read it and he did. He agreed with me. He said: "It has some good writing. There are some vivid characters and situations here, but the script needs a great deal of work." I agreed and we put it in the file with about fifty other scripts.

Then, we had something happen that has never happened before or since. Producer John Golden allowed us to do *Three's A Family* as a vehicle in Harlem while the same show was being done downtown in his theatre. We ran it for about two months, then finally Golden said: "Bring it downtown and show it for one night as a benefit for maybe the Urban League." The *Amsterdam News* promoted the work down there for one performance. We had a packed house and the play went over very well.

Frederick O'Neal was in it as well as Jacqueline Andre, Alice Childress, Ruby Dee, Earle Hyman, Hilda Haynes, and William Greaves, who now heads a film company. But—after this success, we of the American Negro Theatre wanted to go back to original productions.

You see, that was a stunt—a stunt we did because somebody wanted the benefit of that particular show. Although it provided us a showcase on Broadway, it was not our intention to make Broadway our permanent goal. We had to return uptown with another original play.

Yes. We needed a script. And we knew it. We had several in the files, including one by Langston Hughes. I forget what it was called, but it dealt with a hotel lobby situation. I think it was called *Hotel Black Majesty.* Anyway, the group didn't vote for it. The group said: "This is too much old hat and we can't see it."

I said: "I'll rewrite it." And Langston Hughes said we could do what we wanted with the work. We started working on it, but it didn't turn out. We desperately needed a script.

Here we come face to face with the difficulties of theatre being done by committee. Perspicacity rarely wins out. It is ironic that the great Langston Hughes should face this problem with a committee. By the 1940's when the incident described by Mr. Hill took place, Mr. Hughes had won a Spingarn Award, a Guggenheim Award, written a number of plays, and published volumes such as *The Weary Blues, Not Without Laughter* and other books and poems. At just about this time Mr. Hughes had written his highly acclaimed autobiography, *The Big Sea.* Later, after this committee called his work "old hat," Mr. Hughes went on to write the lyrics for the Broadway production of the musical *Street Scene*, with Kurt Weill and Elmer Rice, *The Barrier*, which starred Lawrence Tibbett and Muriel Rahn, *Simply Heavenly, Black Nativity, Jericho Jimcrow*, and the great work involving his favorite character, Jesse B. Semple or "Simple."

Another fact highlighted here is that, despite the Rose McClendon group's search for scripts and the A.N.T.'s search for scripts, one must come to the conclusion that the scripts sought were in the image of the leadership of these groups. Their definitions of what made for a good script became of paramount importance, just as all producers really define what they want to produce.

The scarcity of black-authored scripts mentioned several times must only mean these groups face scarcity in terms of their definitions. What both Mr. Campbell and Mr. Hill should possibly have stated was that there was a scarcity of "their type of scripts."

We started rambling through our files. One day I picked out this *Lucaska* script and I read it on the subway going to my Brooklyn home. I thought about it until about three o'clock in the morning. I said to myself: "This thing has tremendous possibilities."

I called Frederick O'Neal the next morning and I recalled the *Lucaska* script to him. I mentioned that it had possibilities and asked him to read it again. He did, and he said: "I don't know, Abe."

I suggested doing a rewrite on the script and that we put it before the group. The group wasn't too convinced, but there was one beaming-eyed girl who was sitting there, seeing the whole thing unfold. That girl was Hilda Simms.

I had staged *Three's A Family* and I couldn't stand up under another directing assignment. I suggested we find a director and we went down to Pennsylvania, to the Hedgerow Theatre, and talked to Jasper Deeter. He said: "I don't know. I'll think about it."

Then, we went to Venezuela Jones, another director, then to Peter Fry and then to two or three other people. Owen Dodson also turned it down. We had a rough time. So finally I said:

"There's a guy downtown. I saw a production of

his called *Johnny Belinda*—about a deaf mute. That director made the deaf mute articulate. I feel that a man like that can make some of our lesser actors articulate. His name? Harry Wagstaff Gribble."

First, we pursued the Jasper Deeter possibility. He said he would do it, but when it came time to go into rehearsal, Deeter didn't show up. I called him and found out his executive committee at the Hedgerow Theatre voted against his taking the assignment. Taking it would mean making two exhausting trips a week to New York.

So we turned to the idea of Gribble. I had never met him, but I had seen *Johnny Belinda* and I got his telephone number and called him. He said: "Well, I don't know." He was British and very distant. He asked why I didn't get the script to him. I told him the script wasn't ready and that I was still working on it. He asked me to send it to him, anyway. So I sent him the version I was working on. I called him on a Sunday and that man kept me on the phone for three hours. He went wild. He said:

"It isn't ready, but I think this boy has talent. These are vivid characterizations and I think it's a marvelous piece of theatre!"

I said: "Well, thank God! When can we get together?"

He said: "Now, wait a minute. The writing has to be done."

I said: "Listen, we can work it out in the workshop. I don't care how long it takes."

So, I reported this to the committee and the project was approved.

I finally got him up to see a run-through, a rehearsal run-through of *Striver's Row*, which we were reviving for the third time. He sat there and he saw Frederick O'Neal and Jacqueline Andre. He said that he never knew there were such black actors as these people around anywhere. I said:

"Do you think we can cast it?"

He said: "I do indeed."

I said: "Well, I'll work along with you and we'll get together."

So we got together and he was working on that production from the first of March until June, 1944. We got it together and, of course, you know the rest is history.

Now—a mistake was made. In all previous works we were recognized as a try-out experimental theatre by the unions and this allowed certain non-union activities in our set-up. We could use all kinds of talent. And the Dramatists Guild felt an experimental group should get some compensation for "discovering" a script that was bought for a first-class (Broadway) production. I had previously—for former productions with new scripts—submitted contracts to the Dramatists Guild and the guild countersigned these contracts. They read something like this: "The American Negro Theatre will produce a play entitled .... If in the event the play is sold to Broadway, the American Negro Theatre gets 2 percent of the Broadway production and 5 percent of subsidiary presentations, but not including any movie rights." This was understood by A.N.T. When I submitted that for *Anna Lucasta*, I was told at the guild that the lawyer for the guild was out of the country, that as soon as he returned, he would get in touch with me. . . .

After the play clicked, there was much excitement. Gribble was pulling one way and Philip Yordan was pulling another. And I did not have the contract back in my file—the contract I had submitted four weeks before the play opened. After the play clicked, I said: "Oh, my God! I don't have that contract!"

I called the guild and said it hadn't sent me back the contract on *Anna Lucasta.* I was told the guild would check its files. The guild never found that contract.

We opened on a Thursday and the *New York Times* review came out the next day. The news spread all over that A.N.T. had a hit play. The New York newspapers were raving to such an extent that Philip Yordan flew in from Hollywood that Saturday. At the end of the first act, he got up and walked out. I said: "Phil, what do you think?"

He said: "That's not my play."

I said: "I'll agree, because Gribble stuck in a lot of things that I was against, but it's a commercial piece of property." By the end of the third act, he, too, was sold on it. He invited me to have a drink and asked me: "Does the American Negro Theatre want to produce this on Broadway?"

I said: "We are a tryout company. It would change our format if we became a first-class producer. We don't have that kind of backing. I doubt that we would want to change our status on the basis of this play."

Yordan said: "That's all I wanted to know. I brought producers with me."

He had six backers with him. I said: "All right. That's all right if that's the way you want it."

He said: "Now, as far as our contract is concerned, don't worry about it. We're going to take care of you and the American Negro Theatre."

Well, he negotiated with Jack Wildberg, the Broadway producer, and Frederick O'Neal can tell you that Wildberg didn't want to give us a damn thing. I went to Wildberg on several occasions and he said: "Abe, I know what you've done and . . . your dedication and . . ."

Meantime, he's rehearsing and I asked: "Aren't you going to do something before the show opens?"

He said: "Well, I don't really owe you anything, but I'm willing to give you and the American Negro Theatre something." This went on until August 30 and the show was to open August 31. I told Wildberg:

"If you don't make some kind of settlement with the American Negro Theatre, I'll take every penny I've got and get a lawyer to go into court and get an injunction to keep this show from opening!" He stammered and I continued: "I'm telling you, this is it! I've gone along as far as I'm going to go!"

He said: "Well, I'll tell you, Abe—I'll give you a pass so that you can come into the theatre any time free of charge. I will—uh—you bring anyone you like. Since you're working for the *Amsterdam News*, I can pay you a fee to do special promotional work, not only write about *Anna* but go make speeches and. . ."

I said: "I'm not talking about my part. I'm talking about the American Negro Theatre. My executive committee is up in arms because we don't have any agreement and we made the show."

He said: "Well, who's on your committee?"

I said: "Frederick O'Neal. Alvin Childress. . ."

He said: "Well, those people are working for me. I'll tell you what I'll do. I'll give you one percent of the Broadway production."

"We're not going to settle for that," I said. "Those people will tear me apart."

He finally went up to 1¼ percent on the Broadway production only, but no subsidiary rights. He added that he thought he was being generous. I told him I would take it up with my committee and when we met that night, I presented his offer. The committee members said in effect:

"Well, let's take it because we don't have money to fight. We don't have any signed contract. . ."

So they accepted it. Wildberg agreed to pay 1¼ percent and soon afterwards the show was grossing twenty thousand to twenty-five thousand a week at the Mansfield.

Before the opening of the A.N.T. production a separate agreement had been made among Yordan, Gribble, and me that allowed Gribble and me to be collaborating authors. It gave each of us 10 percent of Yordan's royalties. My share was not forthcoming.

About three months after the opening the newspaper *PM* came uptown to do a feature background story. Someone from the *Herald Tribune* came for another feature story. We went out for a drink and they asked for the background of *Anna Lucasta*. I told them everything, including the bad financial deal for the group and no deal for me. A woman from the *Herald Tribune* said:

"Unmentionable, unmentionable!" and after cursing, she added: "I don't believe it!"

"That is exactly what happened," I said.

She told me: "I can't write this story. The *Herald Tribune* won't print it! This man is posing as the Booker T. Washington of the black theatre and you got nothing!"

I said: "When my time came after we had made our settlement, I brought to the attention of the board of directors that I had made a contribution to the script beyond being the director of the group. I had done at least two-thirds of the rewrites."

"Well, you deserve something," she said. "You're union." As I nodded she asked: "The guild didn't back you?"

I said: "They didn't find the letter. They couldn't find the agreement." A second lost piece of paper!

"This is unbelievable!" she said. "I'll have to talk this over with my editor and see what he says because Mr. Wildberg is a great advertiser."

So she talked it over and later she called me and told me the *Herald Tribune* wouldn't print the story. She added that she felt very bad about it and that I really ought to fight the thing. I told her I didn't have any money to fight it. She said she would get in touch with her lawyer—a man named Harry Gilgulin. She did and had me get in touch with him. He said for me to come down to see him. I went down to his office and he said:

"You Abe Hill?"

"I'm Abe Hill," I said.

He said: "What a stupid son-of-a-bitch!"

He went through the case and all the papers I had there. Then he said: "I'll start the ball rolling. I'm going to sue Wildberg. I'm going to sue Phil Yordan. I'm going to sue Claire Leonard. I'm going to sue everybody!"

He mentioned that I had no money and I agreed I had none. He proposed this agreement: "If I go to court for trial, I'll get one third. If I don't get to trial, I'll get one-fourth. How's that?"

I agreed. He took the case and he took about six months fighting these people. They started by offering me $750, then they offered me $1,500, then they offered me $5,000. This went on for weeks and I got sick of these people and Yordan's lawyers threatened to throw me out of the twenty-third story of the Waldorf-Astoria. Anyway, they finally went up to $20,000 so I said to my lawyer: "Look, don't you think I ought to take it?"

He said: "Hell, no!"

It was pointed out that my original contract with Phil Yordan stated that Harry Wagstaff Gribble and I were to be contributing authors. This would allow us 20 percent of Phil's writing, or 10 percent each. But, after we had no agreement, this left us bargaining from no place at all. Anyway, I said:

"Tell them to go up to $25,000."

He offered that bid and he was told: "How do we know he won't jump to thirty?" When the lawyer told me this, I said:

"Tell them they have my word, that's all."

So that's what they settled for: $25,000. But the thing that saved the day was that my lawyer had built his case on the fact that Frederick O'Neal sent a telegram to Jack Wildberg in response to a letter of Wildberg's which said: "Jack Wildberg agrees to pay the American Negro Theatre and Abram Hill 1¼ percent of the Broadway production." O'Neal's telegram stated: "The American Negro Theatre accepts your offer." My lawyer built his whole case on that because it did not say "and Abram Hill"—which did not make me a party to the previously signed agreement.

So, you see, I was playing a dual role. As executive director of A.N.T. I had to struggle to battle Broadway producer Wildberg to see that the A.N.T. earned something for discovering and producing the play.

I also had to battle for the contribution I made to the script as a playwright. After the A.N.T. settlement it was three months before I launched my claim for script revision, being financially compensated six months later.

That's the story of the shenanigans behind *Anna Lucasta.*

Anna Lucasta looms as one of the great tragedies of the American Negro Theatre and the American theatre itself. What Mr. Hill very graciously omitted here is a reality that slapped him in the face numerous times— a reality known to this writer. He was assailed countless times by groups of people because he "found a script and got nothing out of it." These people forgot the very nature of Mr. Hill's organization and that was that his group, the American Negro Theatre, was an experimental group, a community-based institution with no pretensions of reaching Broadway. Countless times the literature of the theatre group underlined the fact that it wanted to tap the untapped resources of the black experience.

But money entered the picture and few people paid any attention to the aims and goals of the American Negro Theatre once the dollar sign appeared. In his own words, Mr. Hill has stated: The theatre became a showcase. Mr. Austin Briggs-Hall, one of the members of the American Negro Theatre, has stated on several occasions that the morning after *Anna Lucasta* was pronounced a hit, there were hundreds of applications from potential professional theatre people who sought to use A.N.T. as a stepping-stone to Broadway.

No words can describe the pain that must have struck at Mr. Hill's heart. Here his group had a commercial success and yet it was not a commercially minded group. Despite these pronouncements, pressure from family and friends exploded into the hearts and minds of Mr. Hill and the membership. It is all a sordid example of people who want to "do their thing," then having commercialism define "their thing" and change its course. Here, indeed, is a mockery in terms of idealism, a victory of the money-grubbers over those who seek a measure of truth and identity—with the victory aided and abetted by well-meaning friends and relatives.

And so Mr. Hill and his group were victims of all of that, and it is understandable, yet regrettable, that he considers himself "divorced" from the theatre.

One shudders at this thought: How many brilliant Abe Hills are divorced from the theatre because of incidents like this? How much is the mediocrity of our theatre and other cultural institutions caused by experiences of this type?

The answer is too painful to contemplate, and yet it must be faced sometime in theatrical history unless we are to continue the course of intellectual mugging of those innocents who walk unarmed in our midst while our theatre continues the vapid course on which it is now embarked.

Several notes should be added to Mr. Hill's remarkable story. One is an interview this writer had with Harry Wagstaff Gribble during the time he was writing the play *Ride the Right Bus* in the year 1951. Mr. Gribble's story does not contradict Mr. Hill's, but differs with his version of these events slightly; both men reveal a bitterness regarding Philip Yordan and Jack Wildberg that is unmistakable.

Mr. Gribble differs with Mr. Hill on their first meeting. He stated that he appeared at the American Negro Theatre with Mrs. Dora Valentine. Subsequently, Mr. Hill asked Mr. Gribble to direct *Anna Lucasta* and Mr. Gribble asked to read the script. After reading it, Mr. Gribble said he got Mr. Hill on the telephone and they talked for hours. Mr. Gribble asked for various changes and when this conversation developed into a discussion between Hill and Gribble and Miss Claire Leonard, the playwright's agent, Gribble states that he saw Broadway.

Hill said he had not thought about Broadway, for his group was community-oriented. Gribble said that Yordan had only thought of his play as a take-off on *Anna Christie*. The sum total, according to Gribble, was that Yordan was to be asked to give *carte blanche* approval for changes in his script. This he gave.

Gribble admitted to this writer that he saw Broadway "all the way." His philosophy then was sharply pro-Broadway not just about *Anna Lucasta*, but about all ventures.

As for opening night, Mr. Gribble had his own Broadway producers there, too, at the American Negro Theatre. When Jack Wildberg entered the picture, the play moved to Broadway and it was billed as "John Wildberg presents Harry Wagstaff Gribble's production of *Anna Lucasta* by Philip Yordan."

Mr. Gribble also said that John Proctor had been of great service to him in rewriting *Anna Lucasta*. This is the same John Proctor, a remarkable theatre man, who assisted Mr. Gribble in later writing *Ride the Right Bus*. Mr. Gribble's association with the American Negro Theatre did not end with the Broadway production of *Anna Lucasta*. He returned to the group and directed *Rain* and *Almost Faithful* and served as an interested consultant on a number of occasions. One interesting production Mr. Gribble wanted to mount was a black-white version of *Romeo and Juliet* with Hilda Simms and a young actor we know well today named Charlton Heston. As recently as 1970 Mr. Heston spoke warmly of that attempt.

The following section is devoted to statements from the recording made by this writer, Abram Hill, Frederick O'Neal, Dick Campbell and Eddie Hunter.

When Mr. Hill had completed his narrative, I noted that his experience had been duplicated many times in the past as witness a case where veteran producer-writer-actor-singer-director Bob Cole had sued his backers for trying to steal from him. I noted, too, that Bert Williams and George Walker had gone to court to sue their managers. Mr. Hill said, sadly:

But there will never be another *Lucasta*. Very few people realize *Anna Lucasta* was one of the longest running straight plays on Broadway. Over 900 performances. Even today it has about the twelfth or thirteenth longest run on Broadway. At one time it was in the first ten.

My mistake was that we had a legal advisor for the American Negro Theatre who thought we were just *playing* at theatre. He didn't take it seriously. He would come in once or twice a month and sit down and hear our problems. He was the one who should have followed through on this contract, but he didn't.

Mr. O'Neal said: You know, the Black Lawyers Group called me not so long ago. They were having a convention in Miami and they said that they would like to have somebody talk to them about theatre law because they had nobody who was really tops in theatre law in their unit. Now, there's only one person I know of and he handled the late Frank Silvera's business. When Frank did James Baldwin's *The Amen Corner*, Frank found out afterwards that he didn't have the foreign rights, the motion picture rights, or any other rights except for the one to present that play in Hollywood and on Broadway. His lawyer just was not experienced enough to come up with it.

After further discussion, Mr. Hill noted some of the playwrights whose work had been produced at the American Negro Theatre. He mentioned Owen Dodson's work, Theodore Browne's, Walter Carroll and *Tin Top Valley* and his own works. There was also a vehicle called *Freight*, directed by John O'Shaughnessy, and this moved to Broadway.

In further discussing the influence of the American Negro Theatre and its heritage, Abram Hill had this to say:

I think the best thing the theatre now still says is that these people, these artists and technicians that came through the portals of our organization have done more to justify the American Negro Theatre's existence because they are living symbols of what we were trying to do. I feel that we made some impact because the theatre in the 1940's was undergoing a transition. Up until the forties, most of the plays on Broadway dealing with blacks were melodramas and comedies and folk plays and musicals and things of that type. But—also in the late thirties Broadway was undergoing a transition led by Clifford Odets, Elmer Rice,

Maxwell Anderson and others. There was a great social revolution underway, the plays of protest, the plays of social meaning, and this was the kind of theatre we were trying to develop. Not just for entertainment and our own professional growth and artistry, but we wanted to say something significant and meaningful to the people. I might say that Dick Campbell's group had a more elite following, but on the other side we were a people's theatre. We would have certain family nights—five members of a family could come in for one dollar. We'd cater to the churches, the schools and groups that would buy out the whole house. Our whole house wouldn't seat but 125 people, but sometimes groups would take two or three nights. We were trying to say something. We were trying to say it within the black media, with the rhythm and the quality of excitement. We had a good teaching staff who worked with our members and really taught them to speak and to project and to move their bodies. We had classes in acting, speech and voice and movement, and we had a technical class for technicians, and we had Lajos Egri, who came in and gave lectures on playwriting. We were really trying to reach within ourselves and say that if the theatre as it exists now is not to our liking, we're going to try and make it so. We didn't even use the word relevant at that time. We said meaningful and significant to the people who would in turn support us because we were giving them a lift and projecting the Negro as a real human being. And this was part of the transitional period in the forties that really finally reached some statement by the sixties. It has all been a kind of continuation of the same thing we were trying to do.

Here, in Mr. Hill's remarkable and very truthful statement, we see what was said earlier in this volume—
that the black American has been caught fighting from
a *defensive* position. It is, bluntly, distasteful to me that
a group should have to defend itself culturally, to
project the reality that "we are also human beings and
dig, Daddy, look what you've been missing." But, if
we are to face the truth, this was the concept from the
Williams and Walker days through the Lafayette
Players, the Crescent Theatre, the Krigwa, the Harlem
Experimental Theatre, the Rose McClendon Players,
the American Negro Theatre and even the groups that
exist today.

Few people are going to like this statement of mine
and a lot of scholars are going to pontificate about this
being the only route to follow. I could not care less
what they think or their various rationalizations. My
only point here is the *defensive* position, the *justifying*
position—and, indeed, the lynching position thrust by
this society down the throats of colored people, Negro
people, Afro-American people or black people. The
nomenclature is really unimportant. What is important
is that in a sense the *condition* of slavery still prevails
and the slave is called upon to justify his humanity.

Frederick O'Neal had this to add to Mr. Hill's
statement:

**We were trying to study various other methods, such
as the Stanislavski method, out of which we would
develop our own particular style. I think in a sense
we succeeded. It would take much longer to develop
it more specifically and coherently, but I think we
succeeded when we consider the time we had to do it.**

In addition to that, I think there is an extension of all these people who came out of the A.N.T. There is an extension in their efforts in the community, in society as a whole today. For instance, you take Earle Hyman. Earle is teaching now. And Roger Furman—he sent me a kid one day and the kid brought in some drawings he had done. Roger had said: "Hell, this kid is better than I am!" I called up Ralph Alswang and told him he had to see this kid's work. Ralph saw some and he got hold of Robert Brustein at Yale and the next thing we knew, Yale had given him one of those never-before-gotten scholarships. And there's something here in what Roger did. It's that kind of extension of the efforts of American Negro Theatre people.

Dick Campbell added: I think there was a kind of natural transition or evolution coming from the Rose McClendon Players into the American Negro Theatre. When my group started, we didn't care whether the play had a message or not. All we wanted to know was : "Did a black playwright write it?" And whatever it was—good, bad or indifferent or pretty bad, we put it on because a playwright can only learn to write if he sees his work done. We adhered to that philosophy. We also tried to develop people. We took a course under Theodore Komisarjevsky and it cost us quite a bit of money. We went down to his studio and we took body movement. We took acting. We also took a course under another director named Harry Coates, but we didn't exactly know what we were going for. We had an idea and we just did what people should do in theatre. We tried to learn, to develop our technique, our bodies, our interpretive abilities and all these things. When the American Negro Theatre started, then they began to look deeper, for other things and—as you say—more meaningful things, and this was a natural evolution.

What Mr. Campbell states here is a valid point. There is also a social-economic-political point that should not be overlooked. The Rose McClendon Players existed during the great Depression. That was the time when various forces looked back for "The Good Old Days." Franklin Delano Roosevelt was in the White House, elected because of his search for a New Deal. In his own words, "The Good Old Days were not so very good for a lot of people." Roosevelt's legislation brought the Magna Charta of labor—the National Labor Relations Act, spearheaded by Robert F. Wagner, then a senator, the father of former Mayor Wagner of New York City. Senator Wagner also introduced the first anti-lynch bill in the halls of Congress.

This, then, was a time of change—a time of considerable upheaval. The Roosevelt policies were in a sense efforts to "patch up capitalism" by borrowing some admittedly socialistic policies—policies which are now ingrained into the American system: The rights of labor, Social Security, welfare administration and pension funds, to mention a few. The American Negro had to benefit on a peripheral basis from these actions, operating as seems to be his wont as an appendage to the American system. The Negro then "invaded" various governmental agencies and these workers became "middle class" or "elitist" as Abram Hill calls them. They were, in all reality, the only ones who could afford to buy tickets and subscriptions to the Rose McClendon Players.

On the other hand, the American Negro Theatre came into existence during the clouds of war that hovered over Europe and burst into World War II. Political activity *had* to involve the Negro then. The dean of the civil rights movement, A. Philip Randolph, launched his threats to march on Washington for fair employment practices in defense plants. This resulted in Executive Order 1102 or the F.E.P.C. There followed Sidney Hillman and his concept known as Political Action; this involved labor operating as a political force. Black people were, therefore, in unions that had previously excluded them, and their incomes made it possible for them to attend theatrical ventures.

Nor can this be minimized. One must return to the reality often stated by composer Edward Boatner that black slaves were freed with "nothing but the rags on their backs."

Dr. W. E. B. DuBois in his *The Souls of Black Folks* speaks of the Negro being a beggar in a land where the dollar is god. This pervasive poverty was to filter down through the ages, to scar the black personality in undreamed-of ways and to keep him eternally outside the American Dream. This pervasive poverty was to put the Negro in the "catch-up stage"—the stage he occupies today where, in the words of Mayor John Lindsay, we are heading for two separate societies and the black one is economically unequal to the white one.

And one is reminded that Langston Hughes once waved his hand in disgust and said:

"The time is never right for Negroes. It is either too early in the season, or too late in the season, or it is too cold or too hot, or it should have happened last year or it should happen next year!"

Mr. Hughes did not say *when* the time would be "right" for Negroes. Only history will answer that one.

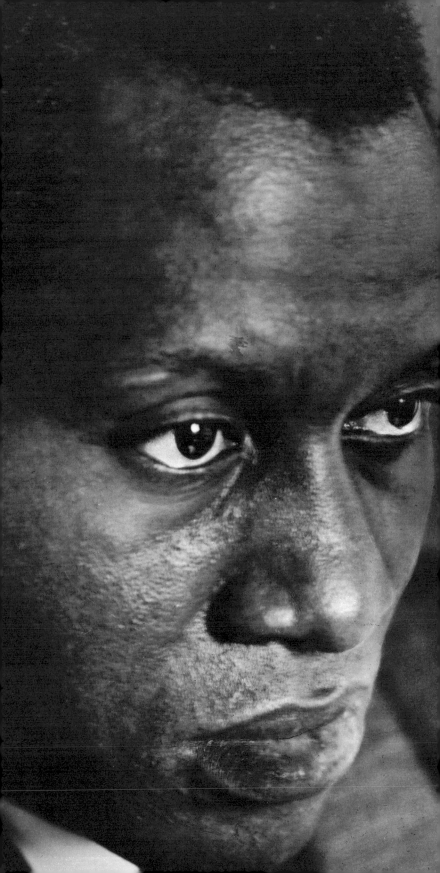

Paul Robeson

Paul Robeson

The following essay was brewed by a storm that struck at a meeting of Actors' Equity Association in 1971. The name of Paul Robeson was mentioned and a young man asked, naively: "Who was Paul Robeson?"

With Frederick O'Neal patiently trying to explain and actresses Osceola Archer and Hilda Haynes screaming, Actors' Equity decided something should be done to lift the curtain of silence surrounding Paul Robeson. A committee consisting of actors Will Lee, Lou Gilbert, Mary Hayden, Miss Haynes, Miss Archer, Louis Polan, Tom McDermott, John Randolph, Mike Kellin, Sarah Cunningham, Earle Hyman, Robert Earl Jones, and Carl Harms, was organized and this became the Paul Robeson Citation Committee of Actors' Equity Association. The committee called on this writer to prepare an essay for the union publication.

With considerable help from Paul Robeson, Jr., and the committee I wrote the following essay for the union publication. Seymour Peck of the Sunday *Times* republished it on August 6, 1972. This circumstance led directly to my contact with my present publisher. This volume grew out of this chain of events.

I am pleased to report that the Paul Robeson Citation Committee still functions; on June 7, 1974, a special award was given to Mr. Robeson. The Paul Robeson Citation is to become a yearly presentation.

When I was a boy in Harlem during the 1920's, his name was on the lips of all my neighbors and friends. They spoke glowingly of this big, handsome, intelligent, brave man who "took nothing off nobody." He was even then a man among men.

From fellow Harlemites I heard the story of his appearance in Eugene O'Neill's play, *All God's Chillun Got Wings*, at the Provincetown Playhouse in Greenwich Village in 1924. This work, dealing with a black lawyer marrying a white woman was published by the *American Mercury* prior to production. Yellow journalism flared. The press wondered if there would be a race riot at the play's opening. But there was no race riot. Paul Robeson very calmly walked on that stage and gave a remarkable performance.

Later, too, he performed the lead in O'Neill's *Emperor Jones*, both on stage and screen. He made a number of films in England and a Hollywood film version of *Show Boat*. But Robeson voiced discontentment and in 1939 he virtually retired from films, saying:

"I thought I could do something for the Negro race in films, show the truth about them and other people, too. I used to do my part and go away feeling satisfied, thought everything was O.K. Well it wasn't. The industry was not prepared to permit me to portray the life or express the living interests, hopes and aspirations of the struggling people from whom I come. You bet they will never let me play a part in a film in which a Negro is on top."

I remember this statement quite vividly. It had a profound influence on many theatre people who simply did not believe Hollywood would ever deal in depth with black America. To this very day, Robeson's state-

ment makes sense for, despite the employment ᴏ̤
actors and black stars by the movie industry in thes̤ᴇ
times, the work being offered is, by and large, "pop"
stuff, superficially "relevant," perpetuating a new stereotype of the anti-everybody black man.

When Robeson left the movies, he continued with
his concert career, ably accompanied by that great
musician, Lawrence Brown. And Robeson was among
the greatest and most successful concert singers of the
twentieth century. Reviews by the music critics for
the *New York World* and the *New York Times* document this repetitiously. And Benny Green, the noted
English music commentator, had this to say of
Robeson: "When he sings I hear the unsullied expression of the human spirit."

While Robeson was winning one accolade after
another, he continued to do exactly what his enemies
disliked. That was the following: He never accepted
his success at the *expense* of the suffering of his people.
Personal success was not enough for him. He demand-
ed success, liberation, freedom, for all mankind. This
demand was *contagious* in terms of the black experience. Its influence was pervasive. In the literary field
we see its influence in men like Langston Hughes not
wanting to be *the* Negro writer but working assidu-
ously to promote other black writers. We see it in Dick
Campbell of the Rose McClendon Players (in the
1930's) and Abram Hill of the American Negro Theatre (in the 1940's) struggling to produce plays by
black writers. In short, Robeson was one of those who
brought selflessness and brotherhood to fellow black
men and women.

An example of this was during the 1930's when he
rallied to the support of the Harlem Suitcase Theatre.

This group, founded by Langston Hughes and Hilary Phillips, produced Hughes's play *Don't You Want to Be Free?* in a loft at 317 West 125th Street, above the site of Frank's Restaurant. The leading role was played by Robert Earl Jones, father of James Earl Jones. Albert Grant, who later directed several of my plays and who is now a lawyer, succeeded Jones in the leading role when the latter joined the cast of a Katharine Cornell Broadway-bound vehicle. Robeson gave the Harlem Suitcase Theatre enough of a fellowship for the group to employ the brilliant Thomas Richardson to work with the group as artistic director on a full-time basis. Richardson, now deceased, had an enviable record of working with community theatre groups and he promptly brought to the Suitcase such talented people as Owen Dodson, Canada Lee and other professionals.

Four years were to elapse before I saw Paul Robeson again. When I saw him again he was starring on Broadway in *Othello*, which featured Uta Hagen and Jose Ferrer. This work, presented during the 1943-44 Broadway season, was the definitive *Othello* of the modern theatre. It ran for 296 performances, an all-time record for any Shakespearean play on Broadway. Robeson won the Donaldson Award for the best acting performance in 1944 and the Gold Medal Award for the best diction in the American theatre. This latter award, presented by the American Academy of Arts and Sciences, has been won by only nine people since its inception in 1924. There is another feature about Robeson's *Othello* and it goes unmentioned. He was one of the few actors who performed Othello's epileptic seizures on stage. And he was brilliant.

What happened to Robeson as a result of his Othello was a prelude to the terror he later met and the curtain of silence that has been drawn around him.

The absolute inconsistency of the American press played a major role in Robeson's *Othello* experience. Critics at first sang praises of his performance. One prominent columnist lauded Robeson's performance, but uttered the hope that the great star would be cautious in terms of political activities. What the columnist said, in effect, was: "America has done well by you, black Paul Robeson, but you should sing its praises and not remind it that your black brothers are in chains."

The curtain of silence had begun to descend. The reasons for this curtain of silence, for the present-day question "Who is Paul Robeson?" are too obvious to mention. For one thing, Robeson refused to allow his success to obliterate the sufferings of other black Americans. Instead he used his prestige and talents as weapons in the struggle for freedom.

Second, he acted on his convictions. The racist, right-wing establishment, led by governmental forces, now launched a powerful offensive against this black man who did not "know his place."

In 1949, when the Cold War was in full sway, Robeson said in Paris: "It is unthinkable that American Negroes could go to war on behalf of those who have oppressed them for generations against the Soviet Union, which in one generation has raised our people to full human dignity!"

This statement was twisted into deliberate lies. Newspapermen and congressmen quoted Robeson as having said that the Negro would not fight for America.

A parade of black public figures was called upon to denounce Robeson. His answer to those denunciations was majestic: "We are brothers in terror."

In 1949 a Paul Robeson concert was scheduled in the Peekskill area. A nationwide campaign was launched against Robeson by governmental forces and by the mass media. Disruptive forces made it impossible for the concert to be held. A second concert was scheduled and this one was held. There followed what can only be called a "police riot." Two thousand state and local police officers had been assigned to keep order. These officers joined in the mobs that attacked those who attended the concert. Photographs exist of New York State troopers standing beside rock-throwing, jeering, cursing "patriots." This sickening example of "Americanism" grew even more sickening when Gov. Thomas E. Dewey called for an investigation *of those assailed*, not the assailants. Dewey wanted an investigation to determine whether or not Communist forces had used the Peekskill concerts to try out their storm trooper tactics.

From that moment on, the concert halls and meeting halls were closed to Paul Robeson. Any organization that sponsored a Robeson appearance was threatened. This became obvious when, during the early 1950's, a group of Harlem citizens organized a committee of one hundred to present Robeson in concert. Many prominent artists who had agreed to participate were threatened by the powers in the entertainment world to "stay away." And many citizens who did participate were "witch-hunted" on their jobs. I know. I was there.

The Committee of One Hundred launched that concert despite threats of reprisals. The black community packed The Golden Gate and the Establishment trembled. Robeson's passport was taken away from him in 1950 and it was not restored until eight years later—all following a long, worldwide campaign and a Supreme Court ruling. Robeson then went abroad and fulfilled concert, TV and theatre engagements all over Europe, in Australia and New Zealand.

It is interesting to note that Robeson was effectively kept off TV in this country, and this explains in large part why the present generation, a TV generation, may have members who ask: "Who is Paul Robeson?"

In 1963 Robeson returned to America in poor health. He has since retired. Hostile forces, however, insisted on attacking him again. This time the mass media lied again about him, claiming that he was a bitter man who had changed his convictions. Robeson shattered this lie with a press release in 1964 (A press release which the Negro press *published in full*. And the white press completely *ignored*).

Robeson said, "The power of Negro action of which I wrote in my book *Here I Stand* in 1958 has changed from an idea to a reality. The concept of mass militancy or mass *action* is no longer deemed 'too radical' in Negro life. The idea that black Americans should see that the fight for a 'free world' begins at home, a shocking idea when expressed in Paris in 1949, is no longer challenged in our communities. The 'hot summer' of struggle for equal rights has replaced the 'cold war' abroad as the concern of our people."

For the record, his views are quoted here from his book *Here I Stand*, pages 46-48:

"My views concerning the Soviet Union and my warm feelings of friendship for the peoples of that land, and the friendly sentiments which they have often expressed toward me, have been pictured as something quite sinister by Washington officials and other spokesmen for the dominant white group in our country. It has been alleged that I am part of some kind of 'international conspiracy.' The truth is, I am not, and never have been involved in any international conspiracy or any other kind, and do not know anyone who is. It should be plain to everybody, and especially to Negroes, that if the Government officials had a shred of evidence to back up that charge you can bet your last dollar that they would have tried their best to put me *under* their jail. But they have no such evidence because that charge is a lie. . . .

"In 1946 at a Legislative hearing in California, I testified under oath that I was not a member of the Communist party, but since then I have refused to give testimony or sign affidavits as to that fact. There is no mystery involved in this refusal. . . . I have made it a matter of principle, as many others have done, to refuse to comply with any demands of legislative committees, or departmental officials that infringe upon the Constitutional rights of all Americans. . . .

"In the wide acquaintanceships that I have had over the years, I have never hesitated to associate with people who hold non-conformist or radical views, and this has been true since my earliest days in the American theatre where I first met people who challenged the traditional order of things. And so, Benjamin J. Davis is a dear friend of mine and I have always been pleased to say so. And he has been for many years a leader of the Communist party of this country."

This amazing man, this great intellect, this magnificent genius with his overwhelming love of humanity is a devastating challenge to a society built on hypocrisy, greed and profit-seeking at the expense of common humanity. A curtain of silence had to be brought down on him. He had to be kept off TV, maligned and omitted from the history books. Perhaps if we begin to lift the curtain of silence surrounding the accomplishments of Paul Robeson, we may begin to walk down the road towards nationhood and equality.

Frederick O'Neal

A Voice: Frederick O'Neal

The only thing that one can say about Frederick O'Neal is that he is one of the great men of our times.

Indeed, much has been written about this tall, heavy, pleasant human being. Volumes exist that document his age, family composition and other vital statistics. Plaques, certificates, trophies and other awards line his Harlem apartment. To cite these here would be an insult to the reader's intelligence and to Mr. O'Neal's eminence.

That he is a beloved friend of mine is a matter of record. The plays he has starred in that I wrote include the following: *Ballad for Bimshire, Ballad of the Winter Soldiers, The Afro-Philadelphian, The World of a Harlem Playwright* and *Tell Pharaoh*. I could relate a series of anecdotes about this good-natured, intelligent man, but I believe it is more important for me to state here that to each venture, professional and private, he undertakes he brings a degree of class, good taste and humanity. His very presence in a venture brings spirit, drive, cohesiveness and all the qualities that make for solid teamwork. You will have to take my word for that and, if you do not, then ask anyone who knows him. Actress Hilda Simms once put it beautifully in speaking of O'Neal. Hilda said:

"He's a saint and he doesn't even know it."

But one of the themes of this book is the pioneering efforts of men and women and this must be stated here: Mr. O'Neal has lived to see many of his pioneering efforts pay off for another generation.

I met him after he had left St. Louis. That was many years ago. In many areas of St. Louis he had already achieved a remarkable theatrical reputation. His work as Henri Christophe, the king of Haiti, in *Black Majesty*, had brought him a national reputation. When he came to New York City and joined the Rose McClendon Players, many of us were awe stricken, for we knew of his work. I remember quite vividly that we stood around, watching him, afraid to say very much for we knew we were in the presence of a star.

Mr. O'Neal soon broke that down and by soon, I mean in less than one minute. He was a star, but he did not think of himself as a star. He sat around with us, drinking malteds, gabbing and laughing, never once revealing to us what we knew about him. He was, indeed, a regular fellow, interested in every single human being and he was much more inclined to talk about a script that was troubling a young writer than he was to sit on his laurels. Even today one has to push him to speak of his accomplishments. Mr. O'Neal will never qualify as a press agent for Frederick O'Neal.

The above remark is not as flippant as it may seem. In all of his written work, the term "I" is absent to a large degree. He speaks of "we" and this is significant. It was never more significant to me than during the production of *Ballad for Bimshire*. Mr. O'Neal starred in this vehicle with Christine Spencer, Jimmy Randolph and Ossie Davis. Once I heard the advertisement manager for the production discussing an ad with the press agent. The press agent told him:

"Be sure to list Frederick O'Neal's name first in terms of the billing for this show. That's what his agent wrote into the contract. His agent told me that it wasn't O'Neal's idea. It came from the agent who said that if it weren't brought up by the agency, O'Neal would never bring it up!"

I laughed, but I was not surprised.

Frederick Douglass O'Neal. That was the name given to him by his father more than sixty years ago.

His father also gave him another important reality and that was the fact that black people face endless discrimination, but this condition must be used by the black individual for positive results. Race cannot be used as an excuse for failure. In short, one must capitalize on existing disadvantages, be proud of them and seek to explore them. And that exploration will lead in depth to greater realities that will benefit all of mankind.

And so Mr. O'Neal went out into the world to explore, to pioneer. His efforts led him into the theatre in St. Louis, into the Rose McClendon Players in New York City, then into the American Negro Theatre, and later to Broadway and Hollywood. He became the first black president of Actors' Equity Association, a position he relinquished during the writing of this volume.

It is important to note here some of his pioneering achievements. From the time I met him, O'Neal was concerned about the role of the black American in the theatre. He sought full documentation of the reality of the black experience on our stages. But, he also sought another reality and this was one of employment for all ethnic groups. He felt that black and other ethnic groups should be cast without regard to race, creed or color whenever possible. I must admit that I had questions about this and so did fellow-writer Harold Cruse. We feared this tactic might lead to the usurpation of the black heritage in theatrical terms. Mr. O'Neal did not. He felt that because ethnic groups are seen in all walks of American life, theatrical reality would be enhanced by such "integrated" casting. Let the record show that Mr. O'Neal's point was well-made because the use of a black detective in Sidney Kingsley's *Detective Story* definitely enhanced the production. The same may be said of other professional offerings.

Mr. O'Neal's efforts led him into an organization that came to be known as the Coordinating Council for Negro Performers, a group of professional actors who during the 1950's organized to pressure for black participation in the entertainment media.

It seems unbelievable to present-day audiences that there was a time when black people were not seen on television, on movie screens, nor on the stage with any degree of regularity. True, today we turn on television and we see black faces on commercials and in major roles in films. The path to that doorway was a difficult one. It has been stated elsewhere in this volume that the McCarthy era, the 1950's, made being black controversial. White people who had black friends were suspected of being Communist-influenced. And the easiest way around the "black problem" was to avoid it.

The CCNP hit the problem head on and it pressured advertising agencies, producers and managers into what we take for granted today—namely, employment for performers of all ethnic groups.

The council was maligned by well-wishers as well as its enemies. Obviously, the well-wishers thought these were disgruntled performers seeking work. The enemies of the organization hardly needed to state a case.

Nevertheless, Mr. O'Neal and the group continued to fight. And the fight was waged at a time when the only black people one saw on television happened to be ball players. We know that the fight was not in vain. The truth is that the black American artist is working in a medium that denied his existence less than a generation ago!

The comment here is about the right to work and not about the quality of the films and television shows in which the artist works.

And, since we live in an age where the dollar is god, it is important for one to be able to make that dollar. Mr. O'Neal, despite his intense idealism, has made it possible for people to make that dollar and to survive with dignity while contributing their talents for the enrichment of mankind.

THE WORDS OF

Frederick O'Neal

Actually my interest in theatre goes way back to the time when I was about 10 or 11 years old. I had a feeling at that time that I would like to go into medicine and I wanted to do a thorough job of training in that field. I talked to my father about it and he said:

"Anything you want to do, I'll help you do it. The only thing I'll ask of you is that you make the best in that particular field that you can make of yourself." Then, he followed with something I'll never forget as long as I live. He said: "And if you are not successful, it's not because you're a Negro. It's because you didn't take advantage of every opportunity."

This was in Mississippi and I knew enough to know that color would be a barrier, but what he was saying is that it is a wonderful crutch and if you've got it, you'll use it, so throw it away first of all. I've lived to see that crutch and many others used many, many times. I've heard girl students (and boys, too, for that matter) say, for instance: "Well, the reason she didn't give me good marks was because I wear nice clothes."

Now, of course that wasn't the reason. She didn't get good marks because she didn't earn good marks. There is a tendency to blame everything on someone else. We're not honest with ourselves. That's our main trouble.

My father had a little store in Mississippi and right next to his store was a meeting hall, and we youngsters would do little shows there. We would dance and sing and do little comedy sketches, and to advertise the performances we would write on the sidewalk: "Come to the show tonight. Admission: two pennies." We would take our mothers' sheets and hang them up for curtains. There was one old lady—the midwife of the town—and she had delivered practically all of us. She would come to all of our shows. I don't know why. Sometimes I'd look at her through the curtains and whatever we were doing on stage, she would be applauding it like all get out. Then I would look out again and she'd have one of those "what the hell" looks on her face—like this was her penance. Anyway, she always came.

Then, I knew it was going to be theatre for me.

My father died, too, and that killed my opportunities for medicine. We sold our property there. At one time the O'Neal family—including my father's brothers—owned a good part of that town, Brooksville, Mississippi, which wasn't saying a hell of a lot. We sold everything but the homestead and moved to St. Louis.

When I reached there, I discovered that the St. Louis Urban League was doing an original play each year. I joined them and finally did *Black Majesty*, the story of Henri Christophe of Haiti. We got good reviews in the St. Louis *Post-Dispatch* and other papers, but then the author John Vandercook wouldn't let us do it any more. He stopped it because he was going to sell it to motion pictures.

It is interesting to point out that the story of Henri Christophe is the same story that brought furious screams when actor Anthony Quinn announced in 1972 that he planned a film version of the Haitian emperor's life. This is in spite of the fact that Mr. Vandercook thought years ago of selling his work to the movies.

There have been movies made that were based in part on the life of Henri Christophe. Eugene O'Neill used part of the Christophe mystique for *The Emperor Jones*—particularly that section where Jones claims he can only be killed by a silver bullet. William Marshall later played King Dick in the film *Lydia Bailey*, and it is said Christophe's life influenced this work.

Our Urban League group thought it would like to do shows more often than once a year. A group of us organized the Ira Aldridge Players. The group was named for the great nineteenth-century black tragedian, Ira Aldridge.

Mrs. Annie M. Malone made all the necessary arrangements to acquire an auditorium that seated about five hundred people. A lovely auditorium. We produced our plays there. We went to the trouble of getting someone to teach us speech, movement and so forth, but this eventually petered out because our actor-students didn't show up and the instructors resigned.

It was frustrating. I always felt that you need constant training in theatre as well as in any art form. I think you've got to keep at it. Finally, it was Zora Neale Hurston who encouraged me to come to New York.

I stayed in Zora's home for two or three days and then I went to room with a cousin of hers. From there I moved to Seventh Avenue and then to the Dunbar Apartments, then I went into the army and I also got married in 1942.

Before that time I had met Abram Hill. Abe and I must have talked about a theatre group for about six months before we got busy on it. I don't think that either of us thought at that particular time that a group like the American Negro Theatre could come off. It had been tried before. Abe had worked at it time after time and so had I. We had become discouraged, but we took a whack at it. Abe has already told about what else happened.

And that brings us to the end of *Anna Lucasta*. Abe left the group in 1948. Without Abe and a number of other folks, the group went down. I was in London and when I came back we made efforts to hold the group together, but nothing much happened.

People were not really supporting us as they might have. Members who were working outside the American Negro Theatre were not really making contributions to the group. This was all related to the total demise of the organization.

When I came back from London I did my first motion picture, *Pinky*. That was in 1949—the same year my mother died. *Pinky* was followed by *No Way Out* and several other pictures. Then the networks and at least one major studio got wind of the fact that I was doing some work in an area that they didn't approve of. And even now I am not employed by the networks unless it is a producer, playwright or someone else who just insists upon having me. Not too many people can insist on that.

I was told by my agent that one of the things they had against me was that I spoke at a so-called Communist meeting. I asked: "Which one was that?"

I was told that it was one that had been held at the old Capitol Hotel. The hotel is now a YWCA. I do not know to this day whether or not the meeting had been called by Communists, but I do know it was a meeting that was called after a group of actors had done John Wexley's play about the Scottsboro trial, *They Shall Not Die*, on Ninth Avenue. A group of rowdies attacked the actors and the police did nothing but stand by and laugh. When I heard about this, I told my agent: "You can tell them that if this happens again and the police stand by and laugh about it—if the Devil himself is running the meeting, I'll be there."

I added that I could still dig a ditch and do a number of other things, so no one need worry about me. I could take it.

And I had a very interesting thing happen after that. There was a television show coming up that dealt with the construction industry. My agent sent me to the producer's office. The author had told me there was a role that had been written for me.

Well, at the producer's office my agent was told that actors' roles in the script had to be approved by the "people upstairs." Well, the "people upstairs" approved all roles except the one I thought was mine. The word was: "Have readings for this part."

The director wanted me, too, and he kept insisting upon using me. He sent word upstairs that he had had readings for the role and he wanted me. The word came down:

"You are not to use that particular person."

Just that. The girl who worked in the office told this to my agent. She added: "If you ever tell them that I told you, I'm going to deny it all over the place."

It all sounded strange. I went to AFTRA about it. One of the officials there told me he didn't understand it. He reminded me that I had been on a Committee on Minority Hiring with a certain lawyer I thought was rather nice. I was told that this lawyer was the one who made decisions on these matters for "the people upstairs."

"That's why I don't understand it," the AFTRA official said.

I decided I would call up the lawyer and I did. He said he didn't understand what had happened either, but that he would find out and get back to me. In a few days he got back to me, all right, and he said:

"Mr. O'Neal, ha, ha, ha, you know that matter we were talking about? Well, the part is for a West Indian and we had to find a West Indian actor for it."

When the vehicle was finally completed and shown, the actor that did it had his back to the camera throughout the film and practically all the lines had been cut out. I remember watching that show and wondering: What lengths will they go to, to carry out this sort of thing. And over the years many, many actors felt this thorn of being listed as unemployable.

Mr. O'Neal is referring here to an era of madness in American history known as McCarthyism. This was an era that seems unbelievable to many young Americans today. For that matter, it seems unbelievable to many who lived through that era.

Although the senator from Wisconsin, Joseph Mc-

Carthy, gives his name to this period, he was by no means the founder of the era. There followed after the end of World War II a period known as the Cold War, with the United States and Russia principal protagonists. Under President Truman the attorney general and the director of the Federal Bureau of Investigation drew up a list of groups considered "subversive." Most black groups were "listed" and it became dangerous to deal with the Civil Rights issue. Loyalty oaths, the McCarran Act, the Mundt-Nixon Bill, and other legislation directed at least in part against the Communist Party in the United States, and the wide spread use of the term un-Americanism were symptomatic of this period.

The House Un-American Activities Committee flourished and many careers were wrecked regardless of the "guilt" or "innocence" of the individual. Artists who were listed were not permitted to work in movies or on television. A group called Red Channels put out a publication and listed names of artists who had done benefits for "left wing groups" or permitted their names to be used. John Henry Faulk, Canada Lee, Alger Hiss and Owen Lattimore are among the more prominent figures who suffered in this era, and many a film, TV and theatre personality felt the effects of McCarthyism.

We live today with the traces of that era. Much of the racial polarization of today relates directly to the era. Blacks were literally afraid to have white friends and whites were afraid to have black friends.

It should be added here that Dick Campbell has said, bluntly, that Frederick O'Neal could have been one of the great character actors in the American theatre. Mr. Campbell said: "When I think about character actors like Anthony Quinn, John Wayne and all who have made plenty of money, well—! You don't find many actors with Fred O'Neal's talent, physique and intelligence—and he was victimized by the Mc-Carthy era. White actors and black actors were victimized.

"Like the others, Fred had done nothing to be listed. All he said was that black actors deserve an opportunity. All of us were saying that. But, the virtue that comes through in his character and in his life is that—while they did not permit him to make big money—nobody but nobody has achieved what he has in his profession, black or white. He has been president of Actors' Equity Association, which is a pretty healthy job. He served as president for nine years. You've got to be something to hold that job. He is presently the president of The Associated Actors and Artistes of America, the international parent body of all the acting trade unions. On top of that he has become a vice-president of the AFL-CIO. In other words, Fred has succeeded in an area he was not shooting for in the first place. You just can't keep a good man down. You can't keep him from advancing."

Fellow-playwright Abram Hill and this writer agree readily with Dick Campbell. We also had had the opportunity to write works for Frederick O'Neal. He is the type of actor that a playwright dreams of having in a show.

Things are better than they used to be. I believe they will get even better in the future. Now we are bringing black producers into the theatre, into motion pictures and other media. These producers exert a certain amount of control and this, I think, is going to speed

up the introduction of more competent black people on the cultural front. Just a few years ago we didn't have any black television directors. For that matter, we don't have too many on Broadway right now. Nor motion pictures. We have a few, but I think that when the work being performed by black personnel begins to make big money, prejudices will loosen. Whether one likes their current work or not, the quality of it, I'm sure, will improve. I welcome all of this because I think that as time goes on we are going to see among other things a tremendous enrichment of the quality in black writing. People have to go through these phases. It's like, I think, when a person writes out of anger, you are likely to get a lecture rather than a play. But I think maturity brings something more or less of a universal quality. I think this is happening now. It's happened to Jimmy Baldwin and I believe to LeRoi Jones. This takes time. Abram Hill has been writing for a long, long time, and I believe his plays have that type of universal quality. And Ossie Davis. When he wrote *Purlie Victorious*, he had audiences leaving the theatre with their sides sore from laughing. But, outside the theatre, audiences began to think about what Ossie was saying.

One of the main things I have been concerned with since I have been with Actors' Equity is getting more color on Broadway. I don't mean in the sense of all-black shows. That will take care of itself. What I mean is a real commitment to the integration of the Broadway theatre. Now, we have gotten to the point where you can see two blacks in a musical—one male and one female dancer in the ensemble. To me this does not represent a total commitment to the idea of integration. It just simply seems as though someone has said: "My God! We've got this show cast and we don't have any blacks in it, so get so-and-so and so-and-so and bring them in here so we can get rehearsals started."

We have a case before the State Commission against Discrimination right now. Of course, we've been there before. But in the last year we've had an agreement with the producers that our Equity committee will read scripts and make suggestions about where minority group actors might be used. In some cases producers have accepted our suggestions. In most of them, they have not. So—after six months of this we took the matter before the State Commission. The producers—represented by the League of New York Theatres—said:

"Why don't we wait until after the entire season?"

And we said: "All right."

Well, now the season is complete and the record is not any better than it was. As a matter of fact, when you look at the whole season, the record is worse than in the past. We are getting our statistics together and as soon as we have them, the Commission is going to call another session. And theatrical agents are going to be called in because they have not been recommending blacks. This is one source of the problem.

Here it should be mentioned that Dick Campbell had these words to say: "Haven't we been doing that for a long, long time?"

Mr. Campbell's words were not acidic ones, for, indeed, black artistic leadership has been doing "that" for a very long time. Both Mr. O'Neal and Mr. Campbell were in the forefront when it came to correlating facts and statistics regarding the employment of black artists in various media. Many may not know nor care to recall that back in the 1950's there were few black artists seen on television. There came into existence in 1951 the organization known as the Coordinating Council for Negro Performers.

Yes, we were doing it then—and this is the cause of considerable frustration in terms of the black experience on this continent. Mr. O'Neal had frequent articles and essays printed, documenting the number of black actors on Broadway in this season or that. It was also suggested back in 1951 that producers and managers would do exactly what they did twenty-one years later—and that was that a committee should read scripts and suggest actors for roles that were not necessarily black or white roles.

It is here that the repetitiousness of the black experience becomes explosive. How long, indeed, can a group of people continue with the same old game shoved down their throats, before "change within the system" develops into anything meaningful? And the cold truth is, this system is married to *pretended* change—change based upon the Dollar. We have had racial changes in sports, on television and in the movies because these changes are advantageous to the American economic structure.

And so the endless parade of hopes and dreams goes on and on until the long voyage ends with direct and disastrous confrontations.

I still have hope. Today I am trying to get fifty openings funded for apprentices in summer theatres this year. This is where most of our members come from—from summer theatres. But, I would like to have these coming by and large from predominantly black

schools. Apprentices would spend ten working weeks in a stock theatre while receiving credit from their schools for this work. The stock theatre management has said these apprentices would be acceptable to them. That means the producer would pay part of the costs and a grant would pay another portion.

Another thing I'm trying to do is get a theatre named for Paul Robeson. We were talking about that some time ago in our Equity council and one girl asked: "Who is Paul Robeson?" I can understand her ignorance; she was born late. Well, the first thing our committee decided was to get Loften Mitchell to write an article about Robeson for our magazine. Frankly, we would like to have a Broadway theatre named for him. And it would be perfect if we named the theatre where he played *Othello* after him. But, that's named after a Shubert, so we have a hell of a job on our hands. But, I think we're on the road to doing something about that.

Also, a recommendation has been made and accepted by the council and that is to give an award each year to the individual who, during the past year or years, exemplified best the ideals of Robeson. This was spelled out: There may be years when we won't give anything at all because we want this award to have some value. And I want to add, too, that our Committee on Ethnic Minorities includes not only blacks, but Puerto Ricans, Orientals and other groups.

By the time this work is printed, I shall have left the presidency of Actors' Equity. I have gone broke on that job. Some years ago I told Ralph Bellamy: "It costs me around $1,800 a year to be third vice-president of Equity."

He said: "You're lucky. It costs me between $9,000 and $10,000 a year to be president."

He was right. It is not a paid job. I do hope to stay with the International, however. And I hope to produce. I believe one thing is obvious when we review the contributions of my colleagues to this volume: That is the fact that there has been continuity in the black theatre and that it is maintained by black producers presenting their fellow artists to the world.

This type of theatre has lived on and on and it must continue to live. . . .

27 = 36 last week
37 - 40
1 - 6 Blue Book

Vinnette Carroll

A Voice: Vinnette Carroll

Each time I think of Vinnette Carroll, I am reminded of a story told by Ed Wilson, the eminent black sculptor. Mr. Wilson spoke of a black American who was driving along a street in the southern part of the United States. This black man drove right on through a red traffic light and he was promptly stopped by a white policeman. The policeman said: "You went through a red light! Didn't you know that?"

The black man said with his tongue in his cheek: "I know I went through a red light. I saw all the white folks going through green lights and I figured the red light was for us." That baffled the officer and he shouted: "Drive on! Just keep on driving!"

And the black man drove off without getting a ticket.

I suspect the story brings Vinnette Carroll to mind because she has never stopped for a red light nor a closed door. She has, in fact, a genius for charging through lights, stop signs and doors that would make others stop and ponder. In short, she does not know the meaning of giving up. And this is one of the qualities that has brought her into the front ranks of theatrical pioneers.

I do not know exactly when I first met Vinnette Carroll and I am certain she cannot remember. Such things are of little importance to her unless one is dealing in dramatic terms. Then she can tell you when two people should have met, why they met or did not meet, and what went on socially, politically, economically and emotionally. When she gets inside the theatre no police officer is going to stop her.

I have fond memories of an occasion in the 1950's. I was sitting in my Harlem apartment, talking with Andrew M. Burris when the telephone rang. The caller was a playwright named Hugh Hill, who had been a fellow college student of mine. He planned to go into law, but somehow he ended up in the Yale Drama School. Hugh mentioned to me that he had written a play called *Song for A Broken Horn*, and he went on to state that he was having trouble casting it for a showing in New Haven.

He described the leading role to me and wanted to know if I knew of anyone who could fill that role. I told him to hold on and I mentioned to Andrew what Hugh had said. Andrew knew more theatre than anyone ever gave him credit for knowing and he promptly shouted at me:

"Get Vinnette Carroll!"

I was ecstatic and I mentioned the name to Hugh Hill. Andrew volunteered to contact his friends, Judge and Mrs. Francis Ellis Rivers, and they would have Vinnette call Hugh Hill. He did just that and not too many days passed before Vinnette Carroll was in New Haven, starring in *Song for A Broken Horn*. And she was brilliant. The reviews and the audience response document that.

But, that success was not enough for Vinnette Carroll. She stuck the script under her arm after the New Haven showing and she went from New York producer to New York producer, urging each to produce Mr.

Hill's play. She met obstacle after obstacle and, unfortunately, Miss Carroll's efforts were in vain. I am convinced that a sensible theatre would have produced *Song for A Broken Horn*. This work belongs to a long list of unproduced plays that make me wonder if we in America are really seeing the best plays that are being written. I know for a fact that many of the plays of mine that have reached the stage appear inferior to those that remain unproduced.

Vinnette Carroll did the same thing with a play of mine that remains unproduced. She carried that play to the Phoenix Theatre when it was on Twelfth Street and Second Avenue. Her argument with the Phoenix over my play was exciting and I have to laugh when I remember the way she battled that organization. She accused it of ignoring vital sections of the American population. Nor did she stop there. She promptly got me into an argument with Marc Connelly, who was vain enough to defend his misleading play, *The Green Pastures*, which for me completely misrepresents the religion of black people. And, to add insult to injury, he also attempted to pontificate about the reasons for the Phoenix reviving Dion Boucicault's terrible play, *The Octoroon*.

Now, all of this may sound as though I am—to put it in Harlem terms—"coming down hard" on Connelly and Boucicault. What I am coming down hard on is the attitudes both express in their work—attitudes that are products of American arrogance. This is the same arrogance that makes Americans of all races wander into foreign lands and try to advise the people of those lands how things *ought to be there*. It is this arrogance that has made our nation unpopular all over the world.

It is this same arrogance that has contributed to the disenchantment and anger known as Black Rage.

Nor is this to be dismissed lightly on an intellectual, international or national level. A careful look at the writers of the world points out vividly how often the black American has had others write about him and for him. And usually this writing has been through white eyes, hostile eyes, know-nothing eyes. One of the troubles with much of the garbage published today about black Americans is that publishing companies hire "Negro experts." These are whites who are in contact with black people and feel that they know them. Publishers are willing to hire them because they—in the publishers' eyes—can see things "white ways" and "black ways."

It is this type of stupidity and arrogance that Vinnette Carroll has knocked down doors and gone through red lights to bring to a halt.

For this reason Miss Carroll had an uphill battle all the way. Snide comments circulated about her, often planted by those she challenged. But, she kept on and the measure of her talent and belief is obvious when one sees her production of Micki Grant's *Don't Bother Me, I Can't Cope*. This production is a tribute to both Miss Carroll and Miss Grant. Both have operated in the open and neither one has compromised at any point along the way.

A volume could be written about *Don't Bother Me, I Can't Cope*, and another volume about the number of awards it has won. It is a smash hit as of this writing—incisive, clean, positive, pointed, lyrical and humorous. Miss Carroll conceived the idea for the production and called on the beautiful Micki Grant to work on it. First it appeared at the Urban Arts Corps, then there were out-of-town showings and, finally, Broadway.

Micki Grant was born with a thousand gifts. She is beautiful, intelligent, kind and understanding. No one in theatre or out of theatre has known her to "put the rap" on any human being. In addition to her acting talents, she writes music and lyrics, and sings and dances.

This writer was privileged to have her in the original production of *Tell Pharaoh* and in *The World of a Harlem Playwright*. It must be admitted here that *Tell Pharaoh*—originally written for a one-night stand benefit—owes its repeated showings because Micki Grant, Ruby Dee, Louis Gossett, Frederick O'Neal, Mary Alyce Glenn and Gloria Daniel, members of the original cast, urged further showings of the work.

Strictly as an aside, this story may illustrate why successful artists must learn to overcome heartaches and disappointments. A play named *The Gingham Dog* was tried out in Washington, D.C., and Micki Grant played the female lead and earned rave reviews. Yet, when the work was brought to Broadway, the producers asked Cicely Tyson to take on Miss Grant's role and Miss Grant was hired as a standby. To put it as gently as possible, the producers were not happy with Cicely Tyson and they replaced her with Diana Sands. It should be noted here that the late Diana Sands took a firm stand and was not going to do the role until Miss Tyson willingly withdrew. In the meantime, Miss Grant continued as a standby.

The play failed. Miss Sands certainly did not, nor did Miss Tyson nor Miss Grant. Miss Sands went on to numerous successes and Miss Tyson's work in the film *Sounder* let the world know of her excellence. And the standby named Micki Grant went on to write and star in *Don't Bother Me, I Can't Cope.*

I cannot resist posing a question here that I know may come back to haunt me. That question is: How many great performing artists have had their hearts broken because we playwrights have not "delivered the goods"?

I am not particularly interested in knowing the answer to that question.

The last time I worked with Vinnette Carroll was when Brock Peters talked us into doing a benefit show for the Arthur Mitchell Dance Studio of Harlem. I wrote the show which was first known as *Come Back to Harlem,* then later became known as *Harlem Homecoming.* Vinnette directed the work and to this date we have not discussed how much it cost us to get this benefit on stage.

But this much I know: Vinnette got it on stage. And she made money for a worthwhile organization.

I started off by telling you she doesn't know the meaning of a red light, a stop sign or a closed door. When you read what she has to say you will undoubtedly agree with me.

And I believe that you will agree that that southern policeman was lucky that Vinnette wasn't driving the car that went through the red light.

I can imagine what she would have told that cop!

THE WORDS OF
Vinnette Carroll

My introduction to the theatre came when I was very young. I used to do recitations at my mother's clubs and in the church. My mother was an extremely cultivated, civilized woman who wanted a lot for her children. She thought it was important to be rounded and to be aware of literature, to be aware of all the arts and to play on our gentler human strings.

She felt this was important because she knew these things would sustain one in life. These were the *inner* things. The other things—the material things—you could lose. We were taught never to become so involved in material possessions that we couldn't function, for to do so would be the very end. We youngsters took music lessons. I took violin and viola and my sister took piano, but there was an enormous pull. My father was—and still is—a dentist and he wanted us to become doctors. But, that wasn't going to be.

That was in New York City, where I was born. But, when I was three and my sister, Dorothy, was four, we went to live in Jamaica, West Indies, with my grandparents. My father and mother married very young. They were both about twenty. In order for my father to go to school, we lived with my grandparents and I didn't return to New York until I was twelve. To a large extent I consider myself West Indian in spite of the fact that I was born here.

Anyway, I went and got my bachelor's degree and my master's and then, to satisfy my father, did all the work for my Ph. D. in psychology. You see, I compromised. I knew I'd never be a physician, the profession he wished for me, because the sight of blood bothered me, so I chose clinical psychology.

The compromise helped in every area concerned. My father thought you ought to render service to make a living and in the arts you couldn't. That, for him, was something you did on the side. My father said the thing to do was to be solvent. A Victorian gentleman, you know. My mother was really very encouraging. I went into psychology and—after about five years—I decided just about the time I was to finish my thesis that if I didn't make the change and go into the theatre, I would never do it. I would spend the rest of my life regretting it, so I went.

I got a scholarship with Erwin Piscator at the New School. I took night classes while I was a psychologist in the day. And that's how it all started.

Evening at the New School was the most illuminating, exciting time for me and while it was happening, I was aware that it was happening. That, to me, was most marvelous because that is something I find that I work on even now—enjoying the experience while it is happening. It's hard to do that and not look back and say: Why didn't I remember how marvelous that was?

I find myself doing that about age: Why didn't I realize I was young when I was young?

At the time of the New School workshop I was twenty-five. You see, I was already into psychology so that meant I would have to take nine hours of dance a week, do all the voice and diction and try to catch up really on the younger people. This was right after the war, World War II.

And I had to study the classics. Piscator was marvelous. We led a disciplined life and it was my whole life. It really was. And I acted a lot in those days, I did Sartre, Shakespeare, T. S. Eliot and others. In school the first thing I did was a part in *The Flies* and

I was also in a production of *Agamemnon.* And how I look back at it now!

The older I got, the harder it got. It's amazing! I went on to my first professional job—Ftatateeta in *Caesar and Cleopatra* for Richard Aldrich. We toured the summer circuit. That was a marvelous experience for me because Richard Aldrich and Cedric Hardwicke wanted me to do it. I remember some people being upset about my being cast in that role. Someone who saw me said to Cedric Hardwicke:

"Can you imagine a black woman is going to play Ftatateeta?"

He said: "Shaw intended that part to be played by a black woman."

It was exciting! I was always interested in the classics. That mother of mine, you know!

I acted a lot of years after that, but then I did a one-woman show. In those days there were few parts for black actors—that is, parts with dignity. My mother used to say: "You pay for everything you get in life and you are lucky if it's money." And I never forgot that and I thought: It's like your dignity isn't for sale and I'm not going to do a part and say: "I'll do this part and make enough money on it and then I'll eventually do what I want to do!" It's never worked. I felt I could never do that so I worked with groups and played all sorts of small parts and then I did a one-woman show for Columbia Concerts. And I got to play all the parts that I wanted to play.

I got the whole thing out of my system! I did what I thought made me get acting out of my system. The economic pressures of the theatre were devastating and I knew I couldn't stay in acting and make a living. It made no economic sense. So—I started to teach at the High School of Performing Arts. I taught for eleven years and it was during that period that I realized that I wanted to direct rather than act. That was a funny time to go into directing because black people were not directing at all.

There was no avenue for a black director. I did several plays for Equity Library Theatre, and then we did a Harlem production of *Dark of the Moon* in 1957-58. In it were Roscoe Lee Browne, Cicely Tyson, James Earl Jones, Rosalind Cash, Clarence Williams III—a cast you couldn't pay for now! It was a special time in our lives. None of us was making it big. We didn't get a penny for our work.

This work was at the Harlem "Y" on its very small stage. We were all idealistic, dedicated, involved, and we rehearsed right around the clock.

We moved the production back to the Equity Library Theatre and then we did *The Disenchanted*. I directed a lot of productions for the High School of Performing Arts. I had no choice. One had to keep on working at one's craft and not depending upon a producer for a job. Nor could one go breast-pounding and thinking: "Oh! Look what you are doing to me! I'll never get a job! Oh, my!"

My mother said the thing one had to do was create jobs for one's self—create the situation where it would make it possible for you to keep on working. So— after I did all those plays at Performing Arts, I went to the Association of Producing Artists (APA) and directed Sartre's *The Flies* for them. Then I went to Los Angeles and directed another production of *The Flies* and *Slow Dance on the Killing Ground* and then things got easier—if easier is the word. It just seemed as though this was the breakthrough.

That was in the middle 1960's. I did *The Flies* for

the APA in Ann Arbor, Michigan, when the APA company went up there. And people began to pay me for my work.

Now I have been asked whether or not I was thinking in terms of theatre pure and simple during those days or did the black experience have a part in my thinking in terms of advancing the black theatre. I have to answer that this is two-fold and overlapping. The revolution, the whole chain in the black experience, the whole thing of black people liking themselves—the whole thing undoubtedly helped one because it made one feel that it was possible to happen, that it was important that we say things in our way and that rhythm and sounds and ways of working were valid and important. That helped a lot.

But, on the other hand, I came from a family that felt you must work to your capacity. We were achievement-driven. "If there is one A in the class, *you* bring it home." My mother said: "Don't tell me that if you're a woman, you can't make it." You have to work to your capacity and then you deal with all the other things—because when you decide you are not getting it, you will have to try everything before you say "I'm not getting this job because I'm a woman or I'm not getting it because I'm black." So—it never occurred to me in those years that I wasn't going to be able to make it. I do not think in negative terms.

I really never think that I'm not going to get a job because I am a woman or that I am not going to get one because I am black. I feel that I am not aware of it—or personally find it encumbering to my technique and to my work to dwell on that.

Certainly I have felt at times that opportunities were denied me. Maybe, because of my protective coat,

I refuse to get hurt or get so angry that I'm immobilized. In fact, I won't. I work better if I'm angry than when I'm hurt because when you are hurt, you are beaten.

Later I did feel a tremendous need to do black material. You see, when we were kids my mother organized a class and we all knew black history. Every Sunday afternoon in this class we reviewed our heroes and we had a sense of being kings and queens, a sense of self. We always knew about Crispus Attucks and Frederick Douglass and all the people who made contributions to this society. We knew, in fact, that if we failed, we had failed *within.* We made sure there was no failure and that things opened up for us.

It never occurred to me that I was less than someone. It just never occurred to me! That sense of self we got when we were young, those positive images that came from family and friends—these were invaluable.

I came back from the West Coast when John B. Hightower and the New York State Council on the Arts were getting ready to form a ghetto arts program. They were beginning to recognize consciousness and, yes, the consciousness of black art. So, they were forming a ghetto arts program in the New York State Council on the Arts and John Hightower asked me to head up the program. I stayed there for about three years and in that time I saw a number of black theatre groups forming—groups with actors that I had taught at the High School of Performing Arts.

This was before the late 1960's. What happened was that, because of the experience at the New York State Council on the Arts, we did research and we found that groups needed leadership and that if we could give them black leaders, black artistic directors for example, this would be helpful to the development of the groups. Up to then they'd always seen white directors. They had not had the experience of having black leaders. So—we started the Urban Arts Corps and that's the group I head now.

To describe it briefly, it was a pilot program that developed out of the New York State Council on the Arts. It was designed to give young black artists a place to develop their works. It's a program for people who need that "next step," for actors who need to play roles they wouldn't get to play ordinarily. It's a place without which, for example, someone like Micki Grant might not have become *the* Micki Grant. We offered a place where she could do several pieces. We worked and developed in that theatre because we would work on a scene and we would try and try—without the heat of a commercial arena. It is a workshop, absolutely a workshop and a place where you don't have the pressure that you have on Broadway. You have the freedom and interrelation of ideas and this is your job and everybody pours into the same pot until you get the right mixture. And you don't have to be afraid of falling on your face and you get a definition of success that has to do with work, with the energies you are using. And there's no such thing as failure.

It's just learning. You get something out of it no matter how it turns out. That's success: You learn. I tell the kids about our whole feeling about awards: You can't get to measure yourself in those terms—the critics coming and praising your work doesn't make it good. The work was either good or not good before the critics came.

Again, it seems to me that one needs that *inner* thing to keep going in this world. All those things like awards can be taken from you. Money, too. If you don't have something inside you or some sense of self or values that are enduring, then you can be lost. If all your measures are in terms of what somebody else thinks of your work, then you really can't develop.

The Urban Arts Corps is multiracial, but it is primarily black. It is multiracial because we feel the need for an input from other peoples and from other groups. An artist has to have illuminating experiences and he has to grow and he can't just sit in a colony. He has to work with other people because that journey from you to me has to be there all the time. If we can't do it in work then we can't do it anyplace!

I notice with our kids—well, they're kids to me— that they have to work with different racial groups: Orientals, whites, Puerto Ricans and others. We learn from each other, from our different cultures and different rhythmic patterns. And so this production we're doing now, *Step Lively, Boy*—adapted by me from Irwin Shaw's *Bury the Dead* with music and lyrics by Micki Grant—has a multiracial cast performing as soldiers. The other show we're doing is a fairy tale and in this one we have a man trying to get food and clothing for the community and his friends. He has to have different friends and the whole community is multiracial. We feel that's important. We have to find ways of working together.

I think the most important thing we have done is *Step Lively, Boy*—not because it's the piece we're doing now, either. We did it two years ago. That's when we started working on it. It is an anti-war statement, very strong. But, when producers came to the

Corps they only saw *Don't Bother Me, I Can't Cope*. That's light and entertaining.

That's why I decided we should do *Step Lively, Boy* now, no matter what, because if you are an artist you have to deal with some of the serious problems and values and deal with how we feel about war and about our fellow man. We have to deal with philosophical concepts.

Despite my involvement with the Urban Arts Corps, I have managed to do some professional work, largely movies: *Up the Down Staircase* and *Alice's Restaurant*. But, the thing that swallowed up a lot of my time was the various productions of *Cope*—one in Los Angeles, another in Chicago. And we are going to open *Step Lively, Boy* in Philadelphia. And another production of *Cope* is going on the road. I have to get that ready. It has taken a lot of my time.

I have to turn down a lot of professional jobs because I feel my responsibility to the Corps—my responsibility to help develop these young artists. And there is a certain discipline that actors and artists must have and I feel it is more important to help instill that than do a commercial production. I do it because I want to do it. I feel it is more satisfying than a purely commercial production.

Now—in terms of this volume and the artists involved, let me say that I find myself in line with these people. They have contributed to my work. People like Muriel Rahn and Dick Campbell were very exciting to me—Muriel Rahn in *The Barrier* and other works by Langston Hughes. And Langston, of course, had a big, big influence on me. He really gave me my first opportunity to direct because the theatre still hasn't gotten to the place where black directors direct white plays. Now, I don't mean to get to attaching any kind of value to it one way or the other. But Langston Hughes asked me to direct *Black Nativity*. That was the first commercial success that I had.

The work of black artists has consistently fed me, inspired me. Each time one is successful, it makes it possible to do other black works and that's another step. This year we did *Harlem Homecoming*, and I directed that. Coordinated it may be the proper word. I saw the richness black artists brought to the theatre. That helped me a lot.

They inspired me, made me proud to be a part of them. The gospel singers! I'm very much influenced by them. It's such a theatrical form. And the music! It's a celebration of religion the marvelous way. Some of our best singers came from the gospel groups. They got their start in the church.

Actually, I suppose it took the black writer to begin the whole thing because no one else was going to ask you to perform. All the white writers were writing the Aunt Jemima roles and you really had to sacrifice yourself in order to play them. It was the black writer and then came the actor and the director and you had the full cycle. The learning process had to come all the way up, but I think the black writer had to be the first.

Other influences? There was the exciting Paul Robeson! I remember seeing him in *Othello* and feeling proud and feeling this marvelous thing about him. And a lot of writers came up—Lorraine Hansberry and all those people. And there was the spirit that Martin Luther King, Jr., had that inspired me. He had the capacity to endure, to keep moving.

My main interest at this point is to work on plays for the black theatre, but I also want to work on the classics insofar as they help a black actor to develop his craft. As I said before, my thrust at this time of my life is the devotion of my time to the development of the black artist. If the use of white plays will develop the artists of my company, then I'll use them. But I feel a responsibility to help develop black audiences—so I have to do serious, meaningful work and have black kids come to the theatre and feel proud that there are artists for them to emulate. They must feel there are roles they can develop and that it is important for them to work on voice, diction, movement and techniques. We must keep lubricating these instruments. Later we are doing *The Flies.* I am going to do classics because I want them to learn control, to be able to do all sorts of parts, to be judged as artists not by double standards. I don't want anyone to say they are good for black actors or any such patronizing remarks. I am dedicated to that and to black writers who are very good. So—for example, if we are doing Micki Grant's material, I will surround her with the best actors and singers to work on her material. That way she can see the vision and get the maximum value out of the experience. I wouldn't give her material to inexperienced actors.

We are funded by the New York State Council on the Arts, by The National Endowment, by individual contributions and so forth. And we have audiences, electrifying audiences. Black people are seeing images of themselves on the stage and so they come to the theatre. I would say that maybe 80 percent of the audience at the Corps happens to be black. I see them coming and the kids are surprised when they get laughs from audiences involved in the production. They are involved! And they make comments after the play and they talk about it and it is all rewarding for the actors and audiences.

There is now a whole black audience. There was a time when a producer wouldn't think of taking on a play like Joseph A. Walker's *The River Niger.* The producer wouldn't think there was an audience for it. But, now—now with the black theatre parties, lodges and clubs—they'll come to the theatre.

If I had to discuss major changes in the black theatre during my time, I would have to point out the sense of self, that black people feel that what they have to say creatively is important. Black artists don't have to use white criteria for judging their work, and the form doesn't have to be a white form. Forms are now his own and he is more willing to develop his own ways and techniques. I remember when I was a kid, you wouldn't use gospel music in the theatre.

The influence of Martin Luther King, Jr., and other civil rights leaders influenced our artists. We have had talented people for a long, long time, but jobs were not forthcoming and black people wanted to see themselves in the movies and the investors and producers began to see that it was profitable to offer black shows. An article on the recent Academy Awards noted that the Billie Holiday influence in dress was quite apparent. Interesting! Black people have a sense now of the clothes they wear, a sense of pride, a desire to design things in terms of us and our background. We wear African gowns and our hair naturally now.

The future direction of what we call black theatre and its contributions seems to me to be leading toward a more integrated theatre, because if you can integrate and not assimilate, I think you are heading in the right direction. If we can all get to be a part of a more universal experience, we will get to see our similarities more than we see our differences. And the more we are economically and artistically secure, the more we will be able to share our experiences with others, and the more people get to know us. In the black community, for example, with a white person coming to the community—that will be part of our experience and we won't think anything of it.

There will be changes. We see now black people in commercials and once there were none. Everything will get to be easier for all of us. I am very optimistic about that, because the more trained actors and the more trained artists we have, the more they'll be used in just any play. I think in ten years a black set designer might be doing *Follies* or some other show.

It is my hope that the time will come when there won't be any need for the Urban Arts Corps as it is now structured. There will be just a place where artists can work and there will be lots of places where black artists can develop and their work will have a value in the society as a whole. It will be a whole different kind of arena. I think it is important for people to have growing experiences and to profit from the whole society and the whole environment and that we grow past the state where we are nursing our wounds and are obliged to say: We are good! We are good! We won't need that anymore because I'll be able to make a mistake in front of you and you'll be able to make a mistake in front of me and we won't judge a whole race of people on the basis of that.

We'll have much more freedom and we'll all be much more adjusted and richer for this!

Ruby Dee

A Voice: Ruby Dee

Many nights slipped into dawns while young men sat around, trying to find words that might describe Ruby Dee. Such terms as "out of sight," "fantastic," "beautiful," "charming," and "cute" flooded one conversation after another. Inevitably, the young men agreed that she was all of these things, yet she was also "something else." Suddenly, one night a black playwright jumped up and shouted:

"I got it! I got it! She is a *living doll!*"

A living doll. The term clicked. Yet, some of the young men expressed fear that "the term doll might be taken in the Ibsenesque sense." Then, someone wondered if her size might be considered in this description. Naturally all of this led to our own definition of a doll. The reasoning was simple: Since we have to spend our lives defining things for ears that do not hear, we might as well define our meaning for a doll.

A doll, we decided, was lovely, durable, and it could be any age at any time. And a living doll was *alive* and had all of these qualities. It was then unanimously decided that Ruby Dee is a living doll—mature, sensitive, compassionate, giving, loving, yet quite durable and quite determined.

I laughed about this pontificating and polemicizing although I fully agreed with the definition. Miss Dee made the definition a reality when she was—to use her own words—"a budding actress." The buds blossomed and critics began to sing her praises. While the critics were singing, one of those producers who thrive on exploitation offered Ruby a role in a script. Ruby took one look and declared the role was demeaning to black

Americans. She rejected the role outright and she did so in no uncertain terms.

This action brought "oohs" and "ahs." Up and down the streets many a so-called militant second-guessed Miss Dee. Some pointed out the man had offered her some "*real* bread." Others suggested that Miss Dee's action came at an unfortunate time in theatrical circles. It was, they said, the time when casting was complete for that particular season and there were no other roles available to black actors.

Ruby Dee could not have cared less than a damn. She went out and got herself a secretarial job.

I could offer a formidable list of roles she has turned down because they projected black Americans unfavorably. And I know she would disapprove of my doing so, because I know that one thing she feels is that one should not be credited for doing what one *should* do.

Ruby Dee. A living doll from Harlem, U.S.A. She was born in Cleveland into the well-known Wallace family, but she spent her childhood and young adult years in Harlem. She attended public schools, then graduated from Hunter College. She was always interested in the arts. She composed poetry, acted in plays, wrote essays and articles. Some of her written work has been published in numerous journals, and most recently her volume of verse, *Glowchild*, has been warmly received.

I do not remember when I first met Ruby Dee, but I did meet her and that was more important than the whys-and-wherefores of how we met. I knew her as an active member of the American Negro Theatre, and she successfully appeared in that group's production of Abram Hill's *Striver's Row*. She did a number of radio shows for the American Negro Theatre as well as several movies. Some of these were for Powell Lindsay and others for William D. Alexander. I was particularly fond of her performance when Mr. Alexander presented her with Joe Louis in the film, *The Fight Never Ends.* Her scenes with Harrel Tillman and the late Elwood Smith were exciting, illuminating and skillfully acted.

Later a respected and critically acclaimed theatre and film actress, Miss Dee remained forever in touch with her Harlem roots. She came to the 115th Street People's Theatre and appeared in Oliver Pitcher's poetic drama, *Spring Beginnings.* She was surrounded by a marvelous cast that included Austin Briggs-Hall, Teddy Grant, Doris Block, Vinie Burrows and Maxwell Glanville. The late Leslie Jones directed the work.

After *Spring Beginnings,* Miss Dee took over the role of Anna in the Broadway production of *Anna Lucasta.* This role, created by Hilda Simms, later had the services of Isabelle Cooley as well as Ruby Dee. There were several companies doing this show in various places. In fact, Alice Childress in her play, *Trouble in Mind,* has a classic remark about *Anna Lucasta.* When Charles Bettis portrayed a young Negro actor in *Trouble in Mind,* he commented to Clarice Taylor: "I have no experience." Clarice promptly stated: "Just tell the folks you were in *The Green Pastures* or *Anna Lucasta.* All Negro actors were in one of those shows."

Miss Childress' thrust is sardonic and humorous, but it is based on fact. Both plays could claim a Who's Who in the Theatre list. This, as far as I am concerned, is a tribute to the actors *not* the plays.

Ruby Dee's career led her to Hollywood where she and her husband joined Sidney Poitier, Richard Widmark and Dotts Johnson in the film, *No Way Out*, and she appeared in the film, *The Jackie Robinson Story*. After that she returned to Harlem where she played the lead in Ossie Davis' first play, *Alice in Wonder*. This work, coupled with two plays by Julian Mayfield, was produced in Harlem by Maxwell Glanville, Mayfield and this writer during 1951.

She was brilliant in the Howard DaSilva-Arnold Perl production of *The World of Sholom Aleichem*, which was presented at the Barbizon-Plaza during the 1950's. This was the time of McCarthyism when many who stood up for the Rights of Man were "smeared." Miss Dee was smeared, but she held her head high and kept right on about her business. And she kept on blazing her way until she has become a legend in her own time. Her work in the films, *Up Tight* and *Buck and the Preacher* and in the plays, *Boesman and Lena, A Raisin in the Sun, Wedding Band* and *Tell Pharaoh* have brought her constant praise.

She and Ossie Davis were both in the cast of *Jeb* (1946), and later Ruby Dee and he were married. They live in New Rochelle with their three children.

It is a privilege and a pleasure to know and love Ruby Dee. To have this living doll tell her own story here is particularly gratifying.

THE WORDS OF

Ruby Dee

When I was asked to contribute to this volume, I agreed because I know the artists whose work appears here. I did not know, however, that I was being considered a pioneer. Black actors have existed— although mostly denied—long before the minstrels.

I argued over the use of the term, and then I asked in my early morning voice: "All right. So what do you want me to do?"

"Talk about your career," was the answer.

Talk about my career? Well, I hardly know where to start. I can begin by saying that I was born in Cleveland and brought up and attended schools in Harlem. I went to Hunter College and I eased into the theatre. I don't remember saying: "I want to be an actress." I wanted to do some writing. I found myself submitting poems to local Harlem newspapers. I found myself in a basement library theatre.

It was no easier for a black woman to become an actress when I began my career than it had been before my time. But I had the support of an ambitious and determined mother. It was through her I had discovered poetry, and I was encouraged by her inter-est in the theatre. And the sense of pride that came out of my home made me take some stands that I had to take. At the risk of getting into a long discussion with my editors, I am not at all certain that one rates the title pioneer on the basis of doing what one should do readily.

Through a friend I joined the American Negro Theatre in my youth and there I met many of my lifelong friends and associates. One of the first plays I did was Abram Hill's comedy, *Striver's Row*. I had fun doing that show and the whole experience lingered with me down through the years. Later the group did a one-night Broadway stand of a "white play," *Three's A Family*. And later, too, I worked with Abram Hill when he produced a number of plays at Lincoln University in Pennsylvania.

Broadway beckoned and in 1946 I played in *Jeb*. Ossie Davis, who became my husband, played the title role. *Jeb* was short-lived, then for a year I did the lead in a cross-country tour of *Anna Lucasta*. From that I went to Hollywood and appeared in Sidney Poitier's first film, *No Way Out*. This was one of the first films in my time to deal solidly with American race relations.

It was not, however, my first film. I had had a number of roles in films shot in and around New York —so-called Negro films, if you will. William Alexander produced a Joe Louis film, *The Fight Never Ends*, and then Powell Lindsay wrote and directed a number of films that I worked in. But it was *The Jackie Robinson Story* that brought me to the attention of film producers. I had the opportunity of playing the role of Mrs. Rachel Robinson in that film.

One thing struck me during the filming of that work and that was the very fact of working in films. I pointed out to a reporter that one had to act in films to *learn* to act in films. There were no studio contracts for black performers to appear in film after film—to learn the ropes, so to speak. There is a sharp difference between a stage performance and a screen performance. On screen an actor does not have the benefit of working for continuity in his performance. The beginning of the film and the ending may all be shot at the same time. Films are not shot in sequence and it is difficult to sustain a mood unless you know the technique.

Someone once asked about black people kissing white people in movies and I, among many others, wondered out loud about when Hollywood was going to allow black people to kiss black people. You see, lovemaking was one of the early theatrical taboos that faced the black theatre artist. Numerous comments were made by that great artist, Ada Overton Walker, the wife of George Walker, about the public not permitting black people to mate romantically on stage. These remarks were made around the turn of the twentieth century. James Weldon Johnson discusses this further in his book *Black Manhattan*.

McCarthyism was a reality during the filming of *The Jackie Robinson Story*. Jackie himself was called to Washington to refute a statement Paul Robeson is supposed to have made—a statement that Negroes would not fight for this country. Mr. Robeson never made such a statement, but the press said he did and Jackie had to appear before the Congress and say that he, Jackie, would fight for this country. However, what Jackie said was taken out of context completely. And I know that Jackie later was quite annoyed about the whole thing. In his book, *I Never Had It Made*, he let it be known that he would not make such an appearance again.

McCarthyism had black theatre artists in trouble. Jobs had always been hard to get and they became harder for us. Some of us tried to revitalize the Harlem theatre movement and in the process Ossie's first play, *Alice in Wonder*, was produced. Also on the bill were two of Julian Mayfield's plays, *A World Full of Men* and *The Other Foot*.

We opened at the Elks Community Theatre, located at 15 West 126th Street. That was in September, 1951, and despite good reviews, we did not enjoy a long run. We were working against the tide of racism and reactionism in the country. Ossie's play was strong. It dealt with a man who was willing to sell out to the oppressors for a fat contract. And his wife would have no part of it.

That experience brought deep despair to all of us. As I look back on it now, I don't know why we didn't all stop and go into other professions. Most of us had children by then and we certainly needed stable incomes. But somehow we did not give up and today I am glad that we did not.

I tried out for a role in Arnold Perl's dramatization of *The World of Sholom Aleichem*, and I performed in that in 1953 at the Barbizon Plaza. It was a hit, a solid hit, and it was absolutely delightful. There were attempts to "witch hunt" all of the actors and in those days such attempts were very real. They included the fact that if you were listed as pro-Red, then you were not able to work in Hollywood or on television. And this listing lasted longer than most people know. It wrecked many brilliant careers and destroyed human lives. The black artist was already listed because he was black and now he was listed as being Red. Langston Hughes discusses this odd situation in *Simple Speaks His Mind*. When Simple is called before the Congressional committee and cited for contempt, he blandly asks the committee chairman: "When I ride the jimcrow train next time, do I ride in the black car or the red car?"

McCarthyism persisted for a long, long time. And the list remained in existence. A courageous law suit by John Henry Faulk brought the list to an end and Ed Murrow and the United States Army helped bring McCarthy himself to an end. But no one can repair the damage done to human beings, the pressures known to families and the breakup of families that resulted from that dreadful period.

Despite all of this, some major things happened during the 1950's. There was Louis Peterson's *Take A Giant Step*, William Branch's *In Splendid Error* and *A Medal for Willie* and Alice Childress' *Gold Through the Trees* and *Trouble in Mind*. These efforts deserved much more of a reception than they got, but at least some of us were working.

In 1958 Lorraine Hansberry's *A Raisin in the Sun* was announced for Broadway production. Lorraine was a lovely, brilliant writer who died all too soon. The producers, Philip Rose and David Cogan, had their troubles getting the money to put her play on stage. But they persisted and on March 11, 1959, we opened on Broadway. The rest is history.

Later came the movie version of this award-winning drama, and then Philip Rose decided to produce Ossie's play, *Purlie Victorious*. Howard DaSilva, director of *The World of Sholom Aleichem*, guided this work to the stage. We opened to rave reviews, but somehow the box office didn't respond to the reviews. We were fortunate, however, in having Sylvester Leaks and John Henrik Clarke take on the job of arranging theatre parties for us. We had a good run, but we didn't make any real money.

There followed the movie version, known as *Gone Are the Days.* Then there were other movies, among them *Up Tight.* Along with Jules Dassin and Julian Mayfield, I wrote the screenplay and acted in the film. And while I was in Hollywood I did a number of television shows.

My days at the American Negro Theatre and my appearance in Ossie's first play, *Alice in Wonder*, bring forth warm, nostalgic feelings. There was the excitement of doing *The World of Sholom Aleichem*—the excitement of being introduced to a new world of literature, to a world I had a feeling for, but I had never really seen nor read as much about the works of Sholom Aleichem that this production brought to me. And the production also reinforced my belief that what we black artists had sought was indeed attainable —that we could portray the truths of our lives without apologizing to hostile forces. In a strict sense, *Alice in Wonder* was the Harlem counterpart and predecessor to *The World of Sholom Aleichem.*

Certainly Ossie's play *Purlie Victorious* followed in the vein of what we might well call the folk tradition. I cannot state firmly enough what had happened before all of this. There had been a lot of talk about the need for black productions to be "universal," to walk away from native lines. The black artist had been expected to imitate the white theatre artist. And *Purlie Victorious* and other vehicles charted the course where we could deal with our lives in our own terms.

I think one of the great things that happened to black theatre during the 1950's and the 1960's concerned the image-struggle. This demands some explanation: Many of us for many years—and many before us—had long questioned the value of doing plays and movies that reflected white values. Certain things were *verboten* and Lena Younger in *A Raisin in the Sun* points this out vividly when she asks Ruth: "Why didn't you tell them your husband was sick with the flu? That's something white folks have, too. Otherwise, they may think we have razor cuts and all that kind of stuff."

Well, few black people any place want to see razor cutting on stage or offstage. But, there is this: Black people are very, very much human beings with human pitfalls, weaknesses and strengths. We are not now nor have we ever been cardboard characters, and what I began to see in the fifties and sixties was the black playwright dealing with total humanity and literally telling the rest of the world: "If you don't like it, you can lump it!"

In short, the play that dealt with the very, very good Negro was replaced by plays about black human beings. A black man could appear on stage and portray a drunk without all hell being raised in terms of image projection. A black woman could say what she thought about American racism without making other black people shudder. It was a time of realism for the portrayal of black life on stage and screen and I welcomed it.

I am positive that this underscored two very exciting productions in which I have recently appeared: *Boesman and Lena* and *Wedding Band*. The tragedy of the colored South Africans was sharply depicted in *Boesman and Lena*, and it was drawn without apology. James Earl Jones played Boesman.

Wedding Band was written by Alice Childress, an old friend of mine from my days in the American Negro Theatre. This play, set in South Carolina during

World War I, told of a black woman and a white man who were in love but who could not marry because of the laws against interracial marriage in that state. Alice wrote the play in 1962 and we performed it at the University of Michigan in 1965. There we earned rave reviews and my husband, Ossie Davis, optioned the play for Broadway, but production money was not forthcoming. After much travail Alice had the play done in Chicago in 1972 and again there were rave reviews. Subsequently, Joseph Papp brought it to his theatre this past year and there it settled down for a comfortable run. This year he directed a film of it for television.

There is a tragedy involved here that cannot be underestimated. Alice Childress is a splendid playwright, a veteran—indeed, a pioneer. She has won awards, acclaim, and everything but consistent productions. It is difficult to think of a play by a white writer earning the reviews that *Wedding Band* earned in 1965 and then having to wait until 1973 to reach the New York stage.

It proves one thing: We may salute and savor the glory of the black theatrical pioneer, but in a land where materialism is all-important, the real salutes take longer.

EPILOGUE

That great novelist John Oliver Killens spoke once of writing a book about the black community's need for a long-distance runner. In his own words, Mr. Killens likened the black experience to a track meet and pointed out that we are running a relay race and passing the stick from one group to a younger group who will pass it on to another.

This volume is part of that relay race. There are others to come from other typewriters about other pioneers. This relay race man willingly passes the stick on to Clayton Riley, Addison Gayle, Darwin Turner, Peter Bailey, James Murray, Larry Neal, Lenora Clodfelter, Carlton Molette, Hoyt Fuller, Ron Milner, Woodie King, Clifford Mason, Ernest Kaiser, Helen Johnson and others. There is entirely too much to be written for any one typewriter.

This volume does not deal with such vital movements as Douglas Turner Ward's Negro Ensemble Company, the New Lafayette group under the direction of Robert Macbeth and Ed Bullins, the New Federal Theatre under Woodie King and Dick Williams, the Afro-American Studio under Ernie McClintock's direction. Nor does it deal with Mr. Baraka's Spirit House Movers, the Bed-Stuy Theatre under Delano Stewart, nor other groups appearing all over the country. Volumes could be written about the Free Southern Theatre and the active West Coast theatre groups as well as the works of Lonne Elder, Ron Milner, Gordon R. Watkins, Adrienne Kennedy, Charles Gordone, Archie Shep, J. E. Franklin, Bill Gunn and

William Wellington Mackey to mention only a few—writers who make up a vital, dedicated group of black playwrights. I repeat: More than one typewriter is needed.

There is need, too, for the type of bibliography that William Reardon and Thomas Pawley included in their book, *The Black Teacher and the Dramatic Arts*, as well as the compilation on Afro-American Drama, 1960-1972, prepared by Helen Keyssar-Franke for the Afro-American Summer Institute held at the University of Iowa during 1973.

Meanwhile, this volume remains part of the relay race. The work of the pioneers included herein certainly helped to pass the stick along, or—if I may change my metaphor—open doors to the very real present. And I can state here without equivocation that each pioneer is overjoyed to note the upsurge of the black theatre movement.

Each one joins me in saluting those now on the scene and in encouraging those who are about to appear on the scene. We join in saying that bleakness and despair should not and cannot hold back those who refuse to be held back. To quote Imamu Amiri Baraka in his marvelous poem: "We can change things!"

And we have changed things and we shall keep on changing things until there is total victory over the bigots who have relegated a vital part of American theatre to a corner of the American experience. Our very being proves we can change things. Our search for heritage has led other ethnic groups on this continent to search for heritage. Yes. We can change things and we can and we shall survive!

Therefore, we shall soar above the earth and sky,

blazing a trail that lasts longer than comets and stars. We shall soar and survive beyond the depths of despair and in the doing we shall free others of their despair.

I see a hell of an age a-coming.

And that age must come despite those who would hold it back. It must come, for the survival of one segment of humanity is inextricably and inseparably intertwined with the survival of humanity itself!

That is what the Voices of the Black Theatre keep telling the world.

In conclusion, I cannot resist changing metaphors again and remembering something from my youth. We youngsters used to play stickball on the streets of Harlem and the home run was our pride and joy. Later we played baseball in nearby parks and there was one cardinal sin: That sin was to take a called third strike. You had to go down swinging!

The Voices of the Black Theatre keep shouting for its members to swing and keep on swinging.

INDEX